"I am circling around God, around the ancient tower, and I have been circling for a thousand years, and I still don't know if I am a falcon or a storm." Selected Poems of Rainer Maria Rilke (trans. by Robert Bly), San Francisco, Harper, 1981, 13.

A QUANTUM PARADIGM

ARCHETYPAL INTERACTIONISM IN AUGUSTINIAN SPIRITUALITY

By Gary C. Rye, O.S.A., PH.D.

garycrye@me.com

yoslayexpress.co

Chapters

PREFACE

This study is intended to be a handbook for pastoral counselors, ministry formation personnel, and those connected with Augustinian communities, as well as church ministers (clergy, deacons, lectors, ministers of communion, etc.) who are looking for some on-going education in the behavioral sciences (sometimes referred to as "human development"). The concepts I describe can be applied to any person, social group, organization or institution. It's like a "template," which one can use to analyze any person or group, especially from the perspective of archetypal depth psychology. This template is best symbolized and concretized both in the "pyramid" or "solar system" metaphor of the psyche (see power point presentation for that diagram in my website, p. 4 Courses, under "preview." I am not attempting to write academically but rather "popularly" and pastorally.

This paper describes some theoretical notions out of the fields of symbolic interactionism, communication theory, psychology, quantum thought, education, religion and theology, Augustinian Spirituality, and planning. The idea is to get to a holistic quantum way of personal and organizational development that gets all realities surfaced and subject to critical reflection. Quantum thought is included because that branch of physics provides some helpful models that can be used metaphorically to help us understand the workings of the human person, human groups and institutions. Taking a phenomenological approach, one isn't so much looking for logical explanations of phenomena, such as "spirituality," but, rather, holistic feeling responses. For example, does it enhance you; do you feel better off with this or a similar kind of spirituality than you do when you aren't involved in one?

Archetypal Interactionism in Augustinian Spirituality

By "archetypal interactionism," I mean the phenomenon that occurs when any one (interiority), two or more persons are engaged in interchanges of various kinds, that often their archetypes, inner energy systems that coalesce around strong affect (mother, father, hero, ego, shadow, destroyer, etc.), get "constellated." My thesis is that the archetypes give us life and meaning, and particularly when, due to our communities of like-minded people intent upon God, we also experience the flavorings of grace underlying the archetypes. In the chapter on Plato, Augustine and Jung (12), I give a succinct description of what I mean by Augustinian Spirituality. Putting these two concepts (archetypes and spirituality) together is meant to imply that Augustinian Spirituality provides a holistic, quantum context in which healthy and wonderful archetypal interactions may take place (persons of other religious traditions might suggest other spiritualities that can serve the same purpose). The reader will find allusions to Quantum thought spread throughout the paper, with more of a synthesis on this concept in chapters 4 and 7. Augustinian Spirituality has a particular charism, which is that of "community." To flesh this out a bit, when people are living in and out of community, another archetypal energy may well become constellated in them which is that of "wisdom." And wisdom leads to prophecy, which in my usage here means an ability to discern the signs of the times. So what we have is a gift to humanity of a kind of wisdom which we can all well make use of.

My hope is that those who use this study will become accustomed to looking for and identifying archetypal patterns, fields and their derivatives and that they will begin to focus in on the fractal nature of psychic, outer, and sub-atomic space, and organizations so as to see how knowledge of any one area might have metaphorical implications for the others.

The most exciting and energy-filled parts of this project and of the writing have been actually "feeling" archetypes and their fields. In some parts of the paper I have concentrated on identifying archetypal fields and getting a sense about them. Once in a while, in conferring with my colleagues about these fields, I could feel and taste and even intuitively "see" them. If I could get in the habit of doing this and guide educational and other personnel to do the same, I'd feel pretty satisfied about having accomplished something significant.

I chose the Rilke quotation for the cover because I felt immediately reminded of fractals and fields in the comparative imagery of falcon and storm.

As I have focused on summing up my findings vis-à-vis archetypal fields, I have been surprised to learn that the recommendations I've come up with for others apply also to myself, and that my studies have led me to personal confrontations with destiny by way of dreams and other manifestations of synchronicity.

Genesis of This Study

This was originally a study of a housing project, done for a program of the Assisi Institute in Brattleboro, Vermont, on *Archetypal Pattern Analysis*. The present version was composed during studies in Augustinian Spirituality, Rome, Italy, Spring 2012.

I am working mostly with Catholic organizations of different kinds, such as general ministry and diaconate training institutes, school faculties, universities and parishes and their sub-divisions. I have found that in these organizations and among their populations there are two contrasting archetypal systems and their respective fields: patriarchy (patronismo, logos: Newtonian world) and community (collaboration, eros: Quantum world). Related archetypal systems are hierarchy and fraternity, respectively. And while I presume that "hierarchy" is itself archetypal and so an inevitable development in organizations, I hope this little treatise might help nudge organizations and individuals more in the direction of community. Or, to put this even more broadly, my thesis is that our world and its organizations have gone too far in embracing *Yang* values and need to now move more consciously and decisively in the direction of *Yin*. This doesn't imply moving from patriarchy to matriarchy, but rather seeking balance between masculine and feminine energy systems. Presently there is great imbalance and this is proving destructive to persons, organizations and even to the very life of the planet due to the patriarchal tendencies that prefer domination to collaboration. Ecological, feminist and other liberation movements often find common ground in a desire to dismantle patriarchy and help the world and its institutions move more toward collaborative forms of organization.

Accompanying this material, the author has prepared a power-point presentation entitled *Typology, Depth Psychology and Religion,* organized as follows:

> Preface & Introduction
> Personality types and temperament
> Philosophical context
> Jung & his times
> Science & psychology
> Wisdom of the East
> The religious dimension & Augustinian Spirituality
> Archetypes & organizational analysis & Summary

I have done presentations of this material several times and in both English and Spanish, with diaconate formation classes in Chicago and El Paso, and with ministry training and adult ed. groups in San Diego, Los Angeles and also in El Paso and to undergrads at DePaul Univ. in Chicago. In terms of learning, initially that takes place mostly during and as a result of class sessions. This written text serves as a backup and resource for that. The main place of ministry for me is in the classroom. I see the classroom setting much as a psychotherapist might view the consulting room, as a "temenos," a container. This is a safe environment wherein teachers and learners are free to think aloud and even interchange roles. When learning is really taking place the participants in the process can be aware of this physically, emotionally, mentally and spiritually.

This is both a study in the psychology of archetypes and a collection of insights geared to help people determine how to best live and work using a *Quantum paradigm*. This paradigm includes making use of contents from the unconscious and using both the macro (cosmology) and micro (sub-atomic, quantum) worlds as metaphors for the psyche/soul. It also includes an embrace of the divine and the workings of grace.

The Patron

My observations and experience lead me to conclude that one dominant archetype and field in religious and political culture is that of the "Patron." This is a manifestation of the archetype of Patriarchy. This field is characterized by an attitude of concern and care on the part of the authority, and by submission and compliance by the dependent population.

In this "Patron" field, there is little room for centers of power other than that of the person or group in charge. The field is generally and usually benevolent unless this power is challenged in some way. It must be stressed at the outset that people don't decide to set up a Patron field. This occurs because that's what people in a particular culture do. That's how, for example, many church organizations have tended to organize themselves.

Now, since 1965, with the end of the Second Vatican Council, there has been loosed in the Catholic Church and its institutions (such as religious orders), a different spirit or archetype in opposition to the Patron archetype and field. This is the spirit of liberation and empowerment, and this field encourages grass-roots democracy and participation in political processes and favors multiple power centers in institutions. This movement is away from Patriarchy/Patronismo. It is not, however, a movement away from hierarchy, which, since this is fundamentally archetypal, will eventually surface in some form even in groups that want to be completely egalitarian. The patron system, however, is not fundamentally archetypal but, I believe, is an historically and culturally conditioned response, and certainly an essential institution of the Roman Empire. And the absence of patriarchy does not necessarily mean the presence of matriarchy.

None of this reflection implies a critique of moral judgment. It's simply that times change, new winds blow and archetypal fields that once served people and organizations, become out-flanked by others.

I think one would do well to keep aware that the movement from Patron field to Liberation field is inevitable, and so would best act in service of that field which encourages self-development, mutuality, and the claiming of appropriate power for oneself and one's groups and organizations. We are in the midst of a great archetypal movement. In part, this is a movement away from a culture of secrecy toward one with a more open flow of information. However, this movement is both sporadic and conflictual.

The Dominant of this study: *summaries of theories of the social, psychological, theological and quantum sciences, especially concentrating on archetypal field theory and Augustinian spirituality and their connection with Quantum thought, are presented, with a view toward articulating a holistic view of reality and the pressing need to move toward more collaborative ways of being.*

Also by way of a "dominant," what becomes abundantly clear in the course of this study is the elemental conflict between those who are more quantitatively, explicate, measurable-world oriented, and those who are more Quanta, implicate and indeterminate-world oriented. Surely this conflict also takes place internally at times in people who see value in both perspectives but are nonetheless attracted mostly to one side or the other.

Religions can be helpful mediators to individuals and organizations in this regard to the extent that they demonstrate in their organizational management and teachings the legitimate place of both sides of the equation. I think right now, in the present historical context, that religions are to some extent failing in this regard because they have moved too far toward adopting a Newtonian stance. I see hope, though, in religious orders and movements such as the Augustinians, due to their emphasis on the conscious building up of collaborative community structures and a way of life that can serve as a model for our time. Augustinian spirituality with its emphasis on grace is also a contribution to modern culture that we all need so much (as is, e.g., the Sufi movement in Islam).
http://simple.wikipedia.org/wiki/Sufism

Intent

One aim in this thesis is to sum up interaction/relationship as the basic factor in all areas of reality and how any given interaction on the human level involves archetypes. So, of course, I am very curious about archetypes, what they are, their variety and how to recognize them.

I intend this study for people who have some affinity both for symbolic interactionism as an approach to Social Psychology and for religious phenomenology and who are also interested in the practical, personal and organizational application of archetypal theory, such as the personnel of religious formation and training programs, social service agencies, church groups, educational institutions, and religious adult education groups.

I also think that the ideas presented here would provide a good "humanistic" basis for people who wish to be or are actively involved in their religions as ministers in some ways. Also, I have come across many people who don't seem to have a context in which to make sense of their religious beliefs, or they live two or more unrelated lives, seeing their religion or spirituality as somehow hermetically sealed off from the rest of reality. I think these concepts will help them with this challenge.

If religions are going to have a good effect upon society, they are going to have to come to grips with the sciences and with the expressed desire of people for a more holistic and well-integrated paradigm for the world we live in. I think this paper is also a move in that direction.

Acknowledgements

My thanks to members of the Immaculate Heart Community in Los Angeles some of whom have been in effect a focus group for this study, and many thanks also to members of an adult education group of Mother of Good Counsel parish in the Los Feliz area. Down Vermont Ave. from this church is a Sikh temple (Gurdwara) whose members and leaders have shown great hospitality to the Catholic parishioners. I think they are a shining example of inter-religious openness. I've also discussed these ideas with groups of Spanish-speaking people. For reasons I don't quite comprehend, a new holistic paradigm approach seems very palatable to this cultural group. I feel much gratitude toward Dr. Michael Conforti and the Assisi Institute and Seminars, and my thanks and gratitude to my Augustinian community for their moral and financial backing in my educational endeavors in general and this study in particular, and especially to the Augustinian Spirituality Institute at Colegio Santa Monica and the Augustinian Patristic Institute (Augustinianum) in Rome.

I hope I'm making some contribution to concepts and a vocabulary on the basis of which we can all converse with each other, those actively involved religiously and spiritually, and also with those of no religious practice. This is not an attempt to seek some common religious denominator or somehow to water down religious or denominational particularities. Hopefully we're all familiar with the beliefs of our own particular religious traditions. My concern is, rather, to look for some common ground, which is, already "there" in the nature of things and that we might all become more deeply convinced that our common humanity, our sisterhood and brotherhood, transcends our religious differences. I write with that hope and I trust that you, the reader, will share it.

Fascinations: when we pay attention to them, then we are in touch with our energy and, so, the world of the archetypes. In terms of this study, one of my fascinations, which I am addressing, is investigating the "stuff" which lies behind visible reality. A good metaphor for this is the stage of a theater: the sets, the lighting, the actors, etc., are visibly apparent. Yet there's a whole world moving around behind these visibilities, which the audience doesn't see. This is like the interactional world of the archetypes. In this paper, I venture behind the scenes looking for educational, psychological, sociological, religious, scientific and other dynamics which are "backstage," so to speak, of the human drama and which are affecting the actors whether they are aware of this or not. These "dynamics" are archetypes. The historical figures best known for archetypal theory are Plato, Augustine, and Carl Jung.

I find this kind of exploration fascinating. I imagine not all people share this particular fascination but certainly some do and so will find my observations at least interesting and maybe even provocative and challenging. I hope others will be inclined by this paper to look more into archetypal theory and Augustinian Spirituality and apply it to their personal lives and organizations.

A Dream

I am in a classroom together with a few others. Most of the participants are Filipinos. The teacher is someone I recognize. She is very competent and from my experience of her, very much given to exactness and precision. Without revealing how I get to this "translation," I think the dream is telling me to choose with care whatever kinds of educational experiences I get involved with. During the dream the teacher asks me a question. I can't respond because at that moment I am having a mini-stroke and I can't get my mouth to vocalize what I'm thinking.

There's some significant direction for me and maybe for others as well in that dream. As a matter of fact, just the day prior to the dream I was visiting a theological school to check out their offerings. I didn't see anything in their list of courses that appealed to me. And I know that, for many reasons, I can no longer emotionally and physically afford to expose myself to learning or other situations that do not hold some promise of nourishment.

Assisi Seminars

I had been attending for several years a study group on a regular basis in Portland, Oregon organized by the Assisi Seminars and Conferences, a group centered in Brattleboro, Vermont (now Assisi Institute). Both in Oregon and Vermont, I have, in fact, been nourished by their presentations. I am so grateful to have found this source of wisdom, which meets both my needs for nourishment and matches my interests, which is fundamentally to pursue integration between theology, psychology, the new sciences and spirituality. The result is a deeper spirituality and a way to articulate my own faith holistically without needing or wanting to denigrate other spiritualities, religions and faith traditions.

Assisi Seminars and Conferences (Assisi Institute) was founded by Michael Conforti, Ph.D. (Jungian Analyst, teacher and consultant), who continues to head it up. He himself has a unique teaching and learning style, which is very dialogical and experiential. I especially enjoy and appreciate his way of working with dreams. Later in this paper I describe the educational philosophy of Paulo Freire. Dr. Conforti embodies his methodology and takes it deeper by inviting the participants into the depths of dreams and their levels of meaning, and, in particular, toward an ability to "feel" archetypal fields present in dreams and in outer life and so gaining some capacity to deduce what archetypes are at work in the life of the dreamer or some larger grouping. I come away from the Assisi offerings energized and awakened.

For me this is living with depth. I imagine there are others who have been and are being faced with similar dilemmas regarding their callings and continuing education, who have moved into a time of dryness or even a kind of despair and who yearn for something more. I hope the concepts and descriptions presented in this paper help guide them toward nourishment and depth in their life-long quest for wisdom.

Dreams

Since I present several dreams in the course of this paper, it would be helpful to describe, however briefly, a dream theory I follow. It comes mostly from Dr. Conforti. I have also belonged to a dream group that meets weekly for two hours, guided by Dr. Ronald Malashock, Ph.D., and a Jungian Analyst. Here's the theory (basically Jungian): dream symbols have meanings quite apart from the subjective take of the dreamer or of others who participate in looking at them. A particular dream, while usually for the dreamer, might also be for some other or others, and maybe even for a larger group, community or culture.

When you first hear or ponder a dream, try to avoid interpretation. Give the dream time to "percolate." Then look to grasp the intended objective meaning of the several symbols (archetypes), and intend to "translate" rather than interpret them (here moving more into Conforti's approach to dream work). Once that's out on the table, then begin to also bring in the more subjective feelings, intuitions and views of the dreamer and any others involved in the session, always checking with the dreamer to see what seems to "fit." Avoid leaping to conclusions about the need for particular actions you think the dream is calling for. In particularly "big" and/or disturbing dreams, the dreamer might also want to bring the dream to an analyst for a more private session. A dream group best regards itself as a sort of temple of Aesclepius (as a "temenos" or container) and the dream as a message from the divine, which is saying something about the soul and life of the dreamer. As you can appreciate, this approach to dream work is very dialogical and interactional on many levels, both within the participants and between them.

Since archetypes are the most fundamental reality in human life, the basic "stuff" of all interpersonal and inter-group and organizational interaction, to really understand in any situation (including in dream-work), what's going on, we have to focus on archetypes and their meaning. Also in dream-work it's quite tempting to get bogged down in subjectivity, looking for everyone's personal interpretations of symbols, but losing sight of the basic principle that a dream means what it says: there's objectivity there, and archetypes in particular are objective realities.

My procedure in this paper is to consider archetypes as the most basic element of all human interactions and relationships. My conviction is that when people are consciously engaged with each other and aware of the archetypal forces taking "flesh" in their interactions that all parties to the interaction are getting deeply in touch with spirit and soul and so are enabled to grow more efficaciously in the spiritual life. On the other hand, lack of such awareness may well leave people cold and detached or even indifferent to each other, even when the intent is to help further spirituality in some way.

Something similar can be said of archetypes and organizations. If you really want to figure out what's happening in the depths of an organization, in its unconscious, get in touch with its major archetypes as they are being felt and lived out in the organization.

And, similar to being consciously engaged with an individual or a group by way of archetypal energy: if people can do this organizationally, that organization suddenly becomes much more alive and vibrant and ways to heal its "complexes" more clear and available.

The archetypes can be approached in different ways. My preference is to go from the more general to the more specific. So in this paper I treat first the archetypes of the personal and collective unconscious: persona, ego, shadow, anima/animus, and Self; then the psychological functions and attitudes (sensation, intuition, thinking, feeling, introversion, extraversion, perception and judging); then some of the more general archetypal fields and forces such as parent, child, wise person and warrior. Finally, I bring in the twelve archetypes offered by Carol Pearson and John Corlett (Awakening the Heroes Within and Mapping the Organizational Psyche). These are: Innocent (Everyperson), Orphan, Warrior, Caregiver, Seeker, Destroyer, Lover, Creator, Ruler, Magician, Sage, and Jester. Each of these archetypes will be described in the chapters that follow as they are alluded to.

Development

I organize my thoughts in this paper in several chapters and sections: Preface, 1) Introduction, 2) Symbolic Interactionism, 3) Depth Psychology, 4) A New Paradigm, 5) Education, 6) Organizational Development, 7) New Synthesis/New Myth, 8) Communication, 9) Theologies, 10) Planning, 11) Opus Contra Naturam, 12) Plato, Augustine and Jung, 13) Signs of the Times, 14) On a More Personal Note, 15) Conclusion, Sources & Suggested Reading, and Abstract.

In each of the sections I am mainly concerned to show the centrality of interaction/relationship as the basic reality present and how, informing all interaction/relationships, are the archetypes, and somehow informing all reality, including the archetypes, is God's grace. For example, that in group life, psychological life, education, experiences of the divine, material existence and organizational development, the underlying reality is always in some way, interaction/relationship, and that informing and shaping the interactions are one or more archetypes and their fields, or, in the case of matter, sub-atomic entities and their fields.

The logic of this development is that one might progress from the particular (from several theories as articulated in different categories), to one's own experiencing of the same. My desire is not so much to share my own, especially pastoral, experiences, as it is to encourage and facilitate the readers to so reflect that they might be moved to articulate their own pastoral approaches and convictions.

One of the fundamental presuppositions of this paper is that archetypes are to personal and collective interaction/relationships what sub-atomic entities are to matter and that both archetypes and sub-atomic particles share some basic characteristics, such as the Yin-Yang movement of positive and negative, toward and away from, connection and separation (introversion, extraversion).

The new paradigm, I suggest, for tying all of reality together, comes partly from the new sciences. This is a description of all reality as one great web of which everything is a part. The central metaphor is the "holon." This word means that what is present in any one area of reality is present everywhere in the web ("fractal"). I concentrate on demonstrating that the principal content of the Holon is interaction/relationship, archetypes, and God's grace. I am also interested in indicating that the metaphors of religions have in common a kind of archetypal substrate and that when a religious system begins to lose vitality it is because a connection with the archetypal has been lost. This happens, for example, through "dogmatism" and fundamentalism.

In looking around for a quantum paradigm that can prove to be an antidote to patriarchy, I think (and I will conclude) that in the Catholic tradition we can do no better than making use of the spirituality of St. Augustine as the *soul* of a new paradigm. Following in the Platonic tradition (and of great influence on Jung), it was Augustine whose thought provided a vehicle for the transmission of archetypal ideas into European Medieval and Renaissance thinking. The model he proposes for community life, with all its different emphases, is holistic and quantum and provides a good framework for the analysis of archetypes as they impact the life of a community and its members. Such a community may be of professed religious, but it doesn't have to be in order to be the "strange attractor" needed for constelling archetypes that promote a quantum paradigm. deals with strange attractors & fractals in chaos theory).

The most crucial archetype with which to seek relationship is that of the *Self*, the inner spark of divinity and, from a Christian point of view, the Inner Christ. Theologically, the Self is neither God nor Christ, but rather mediates them and experientially is felt *as though* them. And in the final analysis are not these psychic and spiritual realities intended to help lead us toward the divine? And is not God's grace somehow underpinning all this?

Literalism & Fundamentalism

I believe that literalist and fundamentalist mentalities in politics, religion, science or any area of human life, hamper an experiential relationship between the Ego and the Self. This relationship, to be felt as living, requires openness to metaphor, something literalism and fundamentalism have great difficulty with.

Also, I believe that literalism and fundamentalism block soul-development as well. One way this occurs is that the radical fundamentalist gets so defensive and so possessed by the Warrior archetype, that he or she has no spare energy for soul-development. (I am fond of the title of one of the books mentioned at the end of this paper, (Death of a Hero, Birth of the Soul by John C. Robinson), because this title implies that the Hero (Warrior) though necessary at times throughout life, especially for Ego development, may block a person from doing Soul work due to the energy needed to maintain the Hero.

Psychologies of Depth

I also want to stress from the outset that a basic knowledge of depth psychology is becoming increasingly important in the 21st century as a way for people to understand themselves and others in all the complexity of their psychosocial makeup. Of particular importance are the concepts of psychological typology and projection. Lack of knowledge of these factors can lead people to think that the way *they* are, feel and think, must be the norm. Thus, people can become very closed to the possibility that there are many ways to be an individual, some of which may feel quite at variance with one's own personality and style. Not all are extraverts, not all are logical thinkers, and many take a long time to reach closure on things. Also, with some frequency the problems and even moral failures one sees "out there" are frequently more the qualities of the viewer than of the person being viewed. So an education in these things has become crucial for people of our time and helps keep us away from new oppressions of various kinds.

The Quantum World

We live simultaneously in a Newtonian *and* a Quantum world. The Newtonian piece

14

is clear enough: no two objects can be in the same place at the same time; gravity keeps us and all other objects safely grounded; things are "really" there, and if you want proof, hit your foot with a hammer. Thank you Sir Isaac. But we are also living in a Quantum world, a world not of solids and gasses which are predictable, but a world of unpredictability and of indeterminacy where even simple observation and intent can change the nature of things. This is true on the sub-atomic level and it is true on the human level as well. We like to think of psychologists and sociologists and other psycho/social professionals' work as completely *objective*. But we know that's not true. Taking a stance or intent or attitude toward someone changes them in subtle ways at least, and sometimes in major ways. Using a Quantum approach to the phenomenon of religious healing, toward understanding of charismatic phenomena, in ESP and other extraordinary events, helps unveil something of these experiences. Archetypes give us a foothold, a grounding in our exploration of the Quantum world, because they, at least, are objective in their core. So to a great extent, this is a study of archetypes and of their importance in our lives in many different ways. This is a study of patterns and of their organizing principles, the archetypes. It is a study of our "complexes" which are really archetypes which have lost their way and have become stuck somewhere inside a person, not able quite yet to reach the ego and be assimilated.

Another way to speak of complexes is to say that they are archetypes made personal. To use an atomic metaphor, the nucleus of any complex is some archetype, and what gets built up around this nucleus is the personal experience of a person of the particular archetype, like a kind of shell. If the complex is more or less benign or neutral, it possibly won't be problematic. But if it is highly charged and unassimilated to the ego, it may well prove problematic and even become the source of neurosis or psychosis.

We are all familiar with personal complexes, both our own and others.' I wonder about collective complexes, in particular those complexes that move organizations toward patriarchy and so the exclusion of the feminine. I don't think the mere greater inclusion of women in patriarchal organizations will do much to humanize those organizations. Rather, in all likelihood, the patriarchal field will prove so strong that even those women who take on leadership roles in organizations, will tend to introject patriarchal values too and act out of them. What is needed for such organizations is a profound conversion to the Reign of God values of Jesus and thus a conscious and conscientious rejection of an exaggerated patriarchy. Again, just to be clear, to reject patriarchy is not to embrace matriarchy. It is, rather, to seek a balance of both masculine and feminine energies either within a person or within a group or organization. And it would not be accurate to equate the patriarchal with maleness or the rejection of patriarchy with femaleness. Nor does a rejection of patriarchy imply a rejection of hierarchical management or authority structures.

This is not to suggest that organizations should not have women in leadership roles. It *is* to suggest that organizations themselves need to so evolve that they consciously adopt a balance of masculine and feminine energies and thus move away from incarnating and acting out of patriarchal patterns. An example of patriarchal patterns would be the tendency to reward those who don't make waves or in any way critique authority. This is a carryover, for example, into Christianity of the old Roman system of patronage. The Empire depended on patronage for its very existence but the churches are not in the same boat. To continue the boat metaphor, it's time for the churches to throw patriarchy and patronage overboard. Maybe the inclusion of women in church leadership roles will help bring this about.

The idea that in order for substantial change to occur in our institutions such that they become less patriarchal and more egalitarian and collaborative, that it is necessary for women to be in leadership roles in a kind of balance with males, makes sense to me. For while not all women carry feminine, Yin energies, they certainly carry them and appreciate them generally more than their male counterparts. In terms of living out of either a more Newtonian or a more Quantum frame of reference, I don't know for sure if women tend to favor the Quantum side, but I suspect they do since the Quantum world is more within the Yin than the Yang field. But as I wrote above, it's very difficult to move against patriarchal values and an exaggerated hierarchical mindset because this *modus operandi* has been around so long that its field is all-pervasive in Western thought and culture. Most people and their cultures and religions still, consciously or unconsciously, presume that men are meant to rule and that women are meant to be subservient. I don't think we are anywhere near a tipping point in this regard. Those religious systems that have come to see the value of sexual equality would do well to attempt to influence their societies in this regard as at least one way of loosening the stranglehold patriarchal consciousness still has.

Summary of the Project

Mainly I want to show that the embracing and living out of an Augustinian spirituality with its emphasis on *community*, is a substantial way to offset the prevailing paradigm of *patriarchy*, and that there can be an ecumenical and inter-religious application of this spirituality (and there are other spiritualities of a similar nature).

My main focus is on showing the close connection between Augustinian thought and the theories of Carl Gustav Jung and his depth psychology school, and that the conscious working with archetypes is fundamentally Augustinian, provided one grants more explicitly the workings of grace as fundamental to the interplay of archetypes.

1

INTRODUCTION

In this introductory chapter I pose the question I keep asking throughout this paper, "how do things work?" I show the importance of paradigms and how we are now in a time of paradigm shift. I suggest that we tend to adopt from and share our paradigms with those persons we consider part of our "communities." I briefly outline a Christian paradigm which I see as opening out toward the more general paradigm espoused in this treatise. I further suggest that we can be clearer about our paradigms when we perceive and act from a sort of "transcendent" place. I locate the particular academic disciplines out of which this paper is written, and finally, I list my own hopes and reservations as the author of this material.

How Do Things Work?

Most of us would like to have some effect on the world before we leave it. In order to do that, it's very helpful to have a grasp of how things work. I mean, socially, psychologically, physically, and theologically: how *do* things work? And is there some sort of *unified theory* about that? I think there is movement toward a unified theory, and what follows in this presentation is about that. This paper concerns a new field of thought that we can very appropriately call "Quantum Theology."

The popular understanding of words like "Quantum" is as "quantity" or largeness. Yet the word was first coined to denote "smallness," the realm of sub-atomic entities, which act as though in "packages" or "quanta" and whose nature is unpredictable in that sometimes they act as waves of energy and sometimes as particles. So it's a good word to use because we are trying to get a grasp on how everything is related, from the smallest to the biggest, and in every possible area of physical, social-psychological, and spiritual realities. In other words, can we use some paradigm, which ties everything together, and which makes sense? What do all things have in common?

Paradigms

"Paradigms" are mental constructs out of which people try to make sense of how they imagine and speak about their worlds. So we all interpret and talk about how we think, feel and act on the basis of such world-views or paradigms. And naturally we become attached to them and we become disoriented when faced with having to think and act in the context of paradigms with which we're not familiar. We also may become disoriented and confused when our paradigms don't seem to work anymore and when we don't yet have new ones. I think our age is like that: it's as though we are between paradigms.

A paradigm out of which many institutions have been working for many centuries, is that of the "Patron" system or field (patriarchy). That too is changing, and sometimes quite rapidly, in institutions such as churches, political parties, countries, businesses, etc.

As science and technology and the findings of the social sciences change, so do our paradigms. Yet right now, and probably for the foreseeable future, change is occurring too rapidly for most people to digest and come to grips with, so they just take parts of paradigms along with them in their life journeys and simply wait for some consensus about new and complete paradigms.

In part, one's religious tradition provides a world-view out of which to make sense of the world, at least religiously; one might also have a political paradigm, and one or more cultural paradigms.

Some people keep their world-views in separate categories. What I mean by that is, that a person could hold to an outdated view about something (such as creation), while in practical daily life accepting a more modern paradigm. For example, someone might consider women incapable of holding leadership positions in religious institutions, yet finds him or herself at work with a woman supervisor or director whom they respect for her talents and insights. But ask him to transfer that experience to religious leadership and you might get a somewhat schizophrenic response.

Such would happen, for example, if their religious paradigm tells them that women shouldn't hold church positions of authority. And trouble comes because one puts theory ahead of experience. Maybe he or she is also failing to consult contemporary social science and institutional life.

Seeking a common paradigm such as is outlined in this book can help with this problem within particular religions as well as in ecumenical and inter-religious relations.

Community

As you consider this material, reflect on it and check out your feeling reactions along the way. Try to call to mind some of the more significant people in your life whose ideas and attitudes have had an impact on you. And consider whether their impact has anything to do with the kinds of people you like to be associated with in what are called "communities."

I want to use that word "community" this way: a coming together of people who enjoy and/or at least benefit from each other's company, who share some deeply felt values in common, and a more or less same or similar world-view. Ask yourself about the communities to which you relate, why you want to belong to them, and what happens when they gather in various ways. Do you think you share an over-arching paradigm with your most basic community? Are you able to articulate that paradigm?

You might find that you consider yourself part of communities that cross over many "boundaries" of race, culture, religion, political persuasion, sexual inclination, etc. And consider how you feel about "competition" as part of your life in community.

Community means being with some like-minded others in such a way that there is a common goal of growing together as persons in God's grace. As a method of discernment, the members of the community can check themselves out using the archetypes of the psyche and the developmental archetypes as useful tools in the spiritual life. They might also wish at times to do dream sharing. The group engages regularly in common prayer and reflection. Each person seeks a *via media* between action and contemplation. And there is mutual service one to another, and to those outside the community, especially the most vulnerable. So the community is nourished by its interiority and prepared for pastoral work, and each of these informs the other.

Competition

Many of us live very competitive lives in our work world and even in relationships of various kinds. It seems to me, however, that, as valuable as a competitive spirit is in business, politics and sports, it is de-spiriting and unhelpful in community settings. By its nature, competition lies within the realm of "persona" whereas community comes out of the space of "Self" wherein openness, vulnerability and genuineness are presumed values. When a person is acting out of a sense of wholeness (closeness to self-authenticity and therefore to the experienced-as-divine archetype of the Self), one does not feel a need to better or best others; rather, one is simply at home with oneself. Competition arises out of a need to impress or please oneself or others and out of a need somehow to be "better."

A Christian Paradigm

In the Christian scriptures, in the First Letter of Paul to the Corinthians, we read something of the outlines of a paradigm that reflected Paul's insights into Jesus' teaching and being. He refers to the just beginning Christian movement and church as "The Body of Christ." Paul (1Cor. 12:12-12:32) had a vision of the nature of the Christian church that is, I believe, a kind of subset of the paradigm developed and described in this paper.

What I mean to say is that Paul was onto something archetypal (and fractal): that just as all Christians are joined as members of the Body of Christ because they are believers in him, so it is with the rest of humanity: all are joined as members of the divine, as one great human family and as part of one great creation.

I want to make this point here at the outset so that readers who are Christian might come to see how their own specific paradigm fits into a larger picture: that they aren't somehow completely separate from other religious and cultural expressions. I would propose that the same is true for other religions as well: that their own specific paradigms of unity (archetypal in that they relate people to the Self), share a commonality with the other similar paradigms. And if a particular religious paradigm is not life giving to its members and if it is not open to humanity at large, then I would imagine the archetypal dimension is not active, at least not in a positive sense.

Transcendence

I find a Jungian and Augustinian schema helpful for this discussion and I include the following material now in order to contextualize the above. I go into Jung's approach to psychology more in detail later in this paper in general and into Augustine's both in the chapter on Theology and in a separate chapter dedicated mainly to him and to some Augustinian/Jungian contrasts and comparisons. For now I want to emphasize his idea that we each act "out of" certain psychological states: sometimes out of "ego," sometimes out of "shadow," or out of "persona," or out of some complex such as the "child." But some people get to the point of experiencing a sort of "transcendent" state wherein they feel that they are acting out of "Self." This *transcendent function*, as Jung calls it ("Mind" for Krishnamurti and David Bohme, or for others the Buddha nature, or the inner Christ), gives a person a perspective, a kind of inner "place." From this place things can be seen much more clearly and one's own inner state observed and accepted as it is (similar to the archetype of the Sage). A person living out of such a spirit as this would not have much interest in competition in relationships.

This Discipline

The most appropriate academic place for what is being considered in this book is Social Psychology. A good sub-set would be "The Social Psychology of Archetypal Interactionism in Augustinian Spirituality." My own personal concern is to try to understand the "world" better in all its complexity and our place in it. The more a person can do that, the more one is able to flourish psychologically, spiritually and emotionally. Part of that flourishing comes from discovering how things work and adjusting oneself accordingly.

To some extent, this quest to find out how things work yields some learnings about how to protect oneself from the many threats which come one's way both from the environment and from within oneself. In a more positive way, this quest reveals some very specific and even imaginal ways in which and through which individuals and groups can work toward their own wholeness and the healing of human institutions and of the planet.

In a most general sense, Social Psychology is an area of academic specialization within the discipline of Sociology. It studies and aims to shed light on relationships between people and groups and between groups. Quantum Theology is an interdisciplinary focus using the methods primarily of Sociology and Psychology and bringing in findings from other fields such as Theology and Physics (esp. cosmology and quantum thought).

Hopes and Caveats

I think you, the reader, will recognize that much of what you read here has figured to some extent or other in my own experience. My hope is that this little *opus* will awaken some reflections of your own and will hopefully assist you in your own individuation and spiritual growth.

This study is written to be discussed. Thus it is framed as a resource for a course on the subject of religion and psychology. My hope is that it be basically "conversational." I think these are really important concepts and that the major thesis in particular on interaction-relationship and archetypes has tremendous implications for people and their lives and organizations, as does the conviction that we are utterly dependent upon grace.

My main areas of interest are social psychology, religion and spirituality, communication, education, organizational development, planning, depth psychology, theology and archetypal pattern analysis, so, naturally, these figure prominently in the following reflections.

I want to stress that I am not interested in writing primarily for an academic audience. Thus I am envisioning this as more a "pastoral" than an academic treatise. I hope the ideas presented speak for themselves and have their own credibility, and that they can be grasped by both the common folk and the more academically inclined.

This paper is rather heavy in theoretical concepts. Every image has a story. In archetypal interactionist archetypal field theory, one looks at an image in search of archetypes and their fields. Most likely one will first feel or intuit the presence of certain fields and complexes. Little by little the image begins to reveal its story or stories, and then the viewer can begin to get a handle on what the fields are really about, make some reality-based observations and from there determine some recommendations. It has taken the author many years of reflection before coming to see the Patron field (Patriarchy) as the most problematic one in human interaction, and one that is fractal on many different levels.

"Fractal" refers to that phenomenon in nature wherein the same basic pattern can be detected in a wide range of entities. Perhaps the clearest is in ferns. Take a fern stem and compare it to the whole fern; then pick off one little branch of a stem, then a smaller piece of that, etc. You will easily detect a similarity of pattern. The same quality can be found in social groups and situations as you examine them. For example, the paternalistic patron system has been present in many institutions and still is, but due to a multiplicity of factors, it is also disintegrating in many places.

We are called to live in two worlds, and not simultaneously. Rather, we bounce back and forth between the more concrete and measurable Newtonian world of practical concerns and the Quantum world of indeterminacy. I find the notion if Yin/Yang particularly helpful in this regard. And yet any given individual will have a preference for either Newton or Quantum, and each culture as well, and one may well be out of step with one's culture in this regard. I suppose the ideal would be if one could only determine when a situation calls for one or the other stance and conform oneself to this exigency. But most of us live lives far from that ideal and oft times cling either to practicality (Newton) or dreamtime (Quantum) when it's the other that's needed. Whatever one's preference in this regard, it seems clear that herein lies a most basic source of conflict and misunderstanding and an area wherein lots of projection takes place.

I think we are very close here in contrasting the Newtonian world with the Quantum one to the most basic dance of creation exemplified even in the subatomic entities of *Boson* and *Fermion*: the first mentioned seeking closeness and union and the second distance and separation. This phenomenon is repeated most dramatically among people and their cultures, and we can line Fermions up with logos and Newton and patriarchy and Boson with eros and quantum and community. Both sides of the yin/yang divide have their place and their time. However, it seems clear to me that culturally we have become much too bound to the distancing Newtonian way of being and are in great need of eros and community and the more yin values these represent.

Awareness of individuals,' groups,' organizations,' and cultures' tendencies to favor either a Newtonian or a quantum stance, will, hopefully make people more conscious of how these differences can be the underlying matrices of conflict. The goal in communication of any kind is to get coherence at all possible levels and in all possible ways, including having both parties to an exchange be either within a Newtonian frame of reference or a Quantum one. I think the most basic source of interpersonal, group, organizational and cultural conflict and misunderstanding is in this area.

2

SYMBOLIC INTERACTIONISM

In this chapter I describe the sociological theory called "Symbolic Interactionism." I describe what is meant by "interaction-relationship" and how this is fundamental to human group life, of which one particular manifestation is "conflict." Another manifestation, and of a more positive nature, is "collaboration" which I also describe. Finally, I present some ideas on "parenting" as one type of human group life in which "interaction/relationship" more obviously holds a fundamental place.

Blumer

In the mid-1970s as I was studying for a degree in sociology/anthropology, I took a course called "Symbolic Interactionism." The professor was Herbert Blumer, then in his eighties. He had written a book with the same name as his class. I took a lot of courses for that degree but his is the only one that still stands out in my mind. Specifically, what I recall and still find fascinating is the central concept of his course and book, which is that "interaction is the basic unit of human group life." He posed that thesis in contradistinction, for example, to Marxism, which posits conflict as the basic unit.

Dr. Blumer would lecture, without notes, for about an hour and then ask for questions. I wouldn't say that he was "interactive" in his approach but I found myself being interactive in an introverted way. That's because I resonated with what he was saying. Without knowing it at the time, his reflections on human group life had some connection with my own path and my own calling.

I decided, largely due to my fascination with Symbolic Interactionism, to specialize in Social Psychology for my degree in Sociology/Anthropology. This really is one subject area of my delight, both theoretically and practically. And one thing I like very much about the field is that it is very multi-disciplinary. By definition and intent, Quantum Theology is also multi-disciplinary. Now just think about it: interaction is the basic unit of human group life. I have come to the conclusion that as much as I am still fascinated with this concept, I no longer believe it to be true in an absolute sense. Rather I think that it's much more accurate to consider that all interaction/relationship includes as its essence, archetypal movement of some kind. I am thinking of archetypes as colorations or incarnations of one's energy while having their own objectivity. Underlying all interactions: the ebb and flow of the Tao. And, ultimately, underlying all human interaction is God's grace.

That archetypes have objectivity becomes most clear when a person feels possessed by some archetype. Sometimes in angry conversations a person who is sufficiently introspective might come to the realization that it's really his mother or father speaking through him or her: some manifestation of the parent archetype. Or a man might be possessed by his ideal of the feminine (anima) just as a woman by the ideal of her masculine (animus). In a couple's quarrel, a psychologist might conclude that what we have is an anima fighting with an animus.

Interaction

We all live in and out of many kinds of groups: families, peer groups of various kinds, support groups, communities, churches, political parties, etc. "Interaction" means any kind of relating between the people of the group. So in a general way, if you want to determine the health or pathology of some group, go to the interactions. Are they open, honest, respectful and loving or would you choose rather negative words to describe the interactions? I think our own techno-culture is developing in a way that is suspicious of inter-personal interaction. In that way the culture itself is becoming pathogenic and contagious and a counter-cultural reaction is imperative and inevitable.

A specific example of people acting according to their symbolic interactionist nature would be good driving. Each driver is giving clear signals about his or her intentions: they signal when changing lanes, they brake as appropriate, and all the drivers are alert and aware regarding all the other drivers' moves. These drivers are clearly in a symbolic mode and are taking into account each other's perceived intentions and gestures. Contrast this with what happens when drivers are agitated, not checking out each other's intentions, not giving clear indications about projected moves, etc. Driving might serve as a metaphor for life.

Things run so much more smoothly when all the people in an organization or endeavor or family are clear about their intentions and are taking each other into account. And a person "runs" more smoothly also when she or he is clear about personal visions, missions, goals and objectives and about the archetypes bubbling around within and in interactions. And, even more so when one is to some extent aware of and even at times experiencing the movements of grace within and without.

Conflict

I mentioned above that pure interaction rather than conflict (a type of interaction) is the most basic unit of human group life. Nonetheless, human relationships and group interactions are filled with conflict, some of it helpful to life and development and some quite hateful. My own interest in conflict is rooted, I suspect, in my own experiences that move me toward both a certain fascination with the phenomenon and a desire to not get too involved in conflictual situations. The way people deal with conflict is interesting. Ideally, one would gear responses to conflict based on what is needed. Sometimes a person would need to be insistent and unyielding and at other times compromising and accommodating.

But most of us don't live in such an ideal world. Rather, each person has favored ways of facing and dealing with conflict. The more one can be conscious of one's preferences in this regard, the more it is possible to consciously choose a reaction which might need to go against the grain. So maybe you're quite competitive: think about collaborating. Maybe you tend to avoid conflict: try to be assertive of your point of view. Note that in this kind of conscious choosing, a person is *seeking* relationship rather than *fleeing* from it. However, it is possible to engage in avoidance behavior and many people and groups do that when faced with conflict.

I did my Ph.D. dissertation on conflict in a Catholic parish setting. What I thought I was observing as conflict between some of the Hispanic population and the parish priest turned out to be conflict between groups of parishioners and they were trying to draw the priest in on their respective sides. My conviction is that the same phenomenon is repeated frequently in other social settings. However, sometimes conflict can be positive provided the population is sufficiently mature so as not to personalize the conflict and to realize that differences of view can lead to growth.

So: the basic unit of human group life is interaction.

And yet, again, that doesn't seem very satisfying. If there's an interaction of some kind then there's going to be some content to the interaction. What most basically is occurring in any interaction? Archetypes. And you can figure out which archetypes are present in any given interaction by getting a feel for the field and for any complexes being manifested. Sometimes a field is apparent and sometimes one really has to dig and be introspective. If one is having a strong reaction to something or someone, it's quite possible that one is in some field. So you ask what it is you are feeling. Does it feel promising or negative? Are you reminded of some strong emotion or experience you've had before? What images do you connect with the feelings? If you can get a grasp of the field then you can more easily figure out what archetype is active and so more consciously decide what stance you want to take in the situation.

Also, archetypes don't just appear in a void without any rhyme or reason. For example, a person has recently suffered many losses through death. Along comes the possibility of job change or loss and the field connected with death again gets constellated (thanatos).

Collaboration

In church work, I've found the best and most rewarding way to proceed in planning and decision-making is to utilize a collaborative style. That means that all involved in executing decisions and all who will be affected by some decision, need to be involved in making the decision and in figuring out how to implement it.

In a concrete way, for me the most efficient way to reach consensus and agreement on general goals has been the "assembly." As church leader or pastor one invites all parishioners who would like to participate to come to a general parish gathering with the stated aim of planning parish goals or directions. Detailed planning might be left to staff or others who are more closely involved in some program, but eventually all those with a stake in the planning process and implementation need to be consulted.

My experience has been that usually about a hundred people will show up at a parish assembly and these are usually the most active people of the parish. Things can get contentious at times, but as long as the assembly can be kept on track and come up with a few general direction-setting goals, people are happy with the experience and will communicate that with the other stake-holders. Other occasional assemblies to report progress and obstacles can be helpful too.

What's happening in such gatherings, from a symbolic interactionist point of view, is that people involved in a common enterprise are being clear with each other about where they want the institution to go and they are respectfully engaging each other as peers in mapping out a future. This activity produces a feeling of ownership and belonging and fosters a sense of community that becomes almost contagious. In retrospect, I wish I had had a better grasp of the power and importance of archetypes when I was engaged in those parish assemblies. I think that kind of knowledge and the ability to identify archetypes and their meanings for organizational development can help tremendously in choosing good systemic directions. Without knowledge of archetypal theory and how to work with archetypes personally and organizationally, both people and organizations can get sidetracked or, even worse, self-destructive.

One archetype that gets quickly constellated in groups seeking to plan together is that of the "Ruler." That can be helpful to the group provided the people experiencing this archetype are consciously working for the good of the group and institution. If not, they may well be living out the shadow side of the Ruler and simply want to pursue their own power-driven agendas rather than the good of the group. On the other hand, one may find that in some particular organization, there is a Ruler vacuum: no one wants the responsibility that goes along with being in charge, in having some leadership role.

Parenting

Many of the problems which affect people both as children, youth and adults, can be traced to a lack of parental interaction; i.e., to the fact that the parents didn't communicate much either with each other or with their children.

People as members of families, peer groups or work situations, simply have to let each other know what's going on and what their intentions are, at least as these might have an impact on the group or the work. And, of course, what's going on most basically in groups of all kinds, including families, is the constellating of archetypes and their fields.

Freud discovered the phenomenon of "repetition compulsion," for example. In terms of parenting: faulty or downright abusive parenting will tend to get repeated on and by the victim. This can manifest as an authority problem. Every time a person experiences any behavior on the part of authorities, as, for example, in a work situation, which is reminiscent of the early parental abuse, the same feelings surface again: the negative parent appears, and the person reacts accordingly, unless he or she is able to get very conscious of these dynamics and so cancel out the repetition formula.

Often parents seem to forget that their family is also a group of people and that common respect and concern requires involving all the members of the family as much as possible in decision-making and planning for many of the same reasons I mentioned above under Collaboration. If later on in life people are uncommunicative and non-collaborative in their dealings with others, in all likelihood that can be traced to an early family situation wherein that was the norm. If that was the case for you or me, then we simply have to find a way to break out of that behavior. This would be the case when the Ruler archetype of early family history was the negative or shadow Ruler: the tyrant.

The most basic unit of family life is interaction.

What one needs to really know is: what are the archetypes all the different people in a family system are experiencing and what archetypes are getting constellated through family interaction? If one or more family members are just beginning adolescence, what archetypes might be coming into play that are complicating family relationships? Can those be named and considered in a rational kind of conversation? A realization that archetypes and their fields are objective realities with their own traits and life, can help people take a more detached look at them and get some emotional distance from what might seem like overwhelming issues.

Sometimes, for example, a very compliant young man, now just starting high school, suddenly begins to get swamped by the archetype of the Warrior. If he can find healthy ways to discharge and use that archetype, he'll develop in a good way. If he doesn't find healthy outlets, he may be tempted to get into a gang or engage in reckless or even criminal behavior (shadow of the Warrior). Let's say his sister was quite a wild little kid, curious (Seeker) about everything, and suddenly she becomes a Caregiver, something not at all expected by her parents. So this family has a lot of issues to deal with. And if the parents are just getting into middle age and the crises that go with that, the issues get even more complicated. Maybe the father is dissatisfied with his job and really feels inclined to start his own business (Creator) and his wife is getting infatuated with her hairdresser (Eros/Lover).

Now, suppose the family seeks counseling with a family therapist. What qualities would they be looking for in a therapist? One who would be capable of dealing with all their difficulties and their particular collection of archetypes. We'll return to this example in the next chapter.

For now I'd like to speculate that therapeutic movement and healing is more likely to occur in this situation if the therapist involved can be working more out of a quantum rather than a Newtonian framework. What I mean by that, more specifically, is that the therapist have some awareness that observation of these family members inevitably alters their thinking, feeling and behavior. In a Newtonian world, the therapist would likely draw up a concrete plan of intended behavioral outcomes and devise a therapeutic approach which would implement this plan. This approach simply pretends that everything is nicely objective and that the therapist can and must act in a rather detached manner, hoping that cognitive verbal interventions will bring about the desired changes.

A better (Quantum) approach would be to admit one does not have all the answers and rather than follow a pre-set plan, one would explore the imaginal world by asking the question "What is wanted?" Sometimes I go into a bookstore and I'll see a book that gets my attention, one that fits well into my present work and interest. I'm at that point operating out of a quantum mentality or paradigm. At other times I go into a bookstore having a title in mind; I search for the book and if I find it, I buy it most of the time. These are two different ways of approaching reality.

Another example: I go to teach a class. I like organizing my thoughts on power point, which means bringing a projector and my computer and some speakers in case I include some you-tubes. To get organized for the class and to get stuff set up I need to go into a Newtonian framework, which makes me somewhat stressed since it's not my world of most comfort. Once I'm into the content I can become more Quantum-oriented and then dance back and forth between these two worlds as need determines. Some similar approach would be used by the therapist in the example above: exploration with the family of their issues would best use Quantum; an action plan, Newton's world.

3

DEPTH PSYCHOLOGY

In this chapter I describe in some detail certain central concepts of Jungian Psychology, such as "shadow," "psychological functions," and the "hero/heroine" archetype. I also present a brief resume of some aspects of alchemy, of the "ego-self axis," and of narcissism. "Synchronicity" is also an important element of Jungian Psychology, so I offer a description of that phenomenon as well as the "born again" experience. As in the other chapters of this book, the underlying "thesis" is that we are always dealing with interaction/relationship and archetypes whether in social or psychological life, and that when there are disruptions of various kinds in relationships, that it is then that we are presented with pathologies (such as narcissism). I also investigate the phenomenon of "images" briefly and how these are understood as quantum phenomena.

Consider for a moment the psychological. Wouldn't the same principle considered previously in this paper hold true? The basic unit of human psychological life is interaction. Certainly, but again there's always some kind of content in interactions, and that content is most basically by way of archetypes and their fields.

Now to get back to the example from the previous chapter: Some of the qualities this family will be needing in a family therapist, are: the ability to maintain some order during a session (Ruler); the ability to deeply empathize with all the people of the family and feel something of their pain (Caregiver & Magician); the ability to be objective and reflect back to this family what is really there (Sage); and, finally, the ability to see humor even in the most absurd and potentially tragic (Jester). That's quite a collection of talents. I hope they can find someone who can measure up.

In Carol Pearson's scheme of things, the specific archetypes I've been describing in this paper are conveniently divided into three groups: development of Ego, development of Soul, and development of Self. So the sets are: Innocent, Orphan, Warrior & Caregiver; Seeker, Destroyer, Lover & Creator; Ruler, Magician, Sage & Jester. In the family example I am presenting, you can clearly see that the kind of therapist this family needs is a very mature one who is already developing the archetypes of the Self. (Mark & Pearson's book The Hero and the Outlaw presents an application of archetypal theory to advertising).

One important thing to note is that no one simply develops all these archetypes in order and then is finished and completed. Rather each person jumps around as both his or her nature and environment incline them, and they are brought into some archetypal space or invaded by some archetype usually not so much because they want to or plan to, but directed more by circumstances and fate (see Conforti).

Jung

The best-known psychologist in archetypal theory is Carl G. Jung. In his extensive writings, he maps out the human psyche. Each person consists of a multiplicity of inner "characters": e.g., ego, persona, shadow, anima/animus (see Chap. 12), Self (& other archetypes and complexes). These inner figures reveal themselves to a person by way of moods, projections and dreams. Psychotherapy leading to greater individuation, from a Jungian standpoint, takes place when a person interacts with these figures (archetypes); for example, getting into a conversation with the symbolic representations in one's dreams, speaking to them and, in imagination, letting them have their say. This is called active imagination. So I think it can be safely said, "the basic unit of inner life is interaction," just as it is in outer, social life. Now this is universal to all cultures and to people everywhere, which is what a Quantum Paradigm is interested in.

Shadow

That each person has a personal "shadow" with specific contents, which are more or less unconscious, is a constant of human experience. And unless a person is willing to look at those contents and deal with them, they will be "projected " out onto some other person or group. For example, if there are unacknowledged homosexual feelings and urges: in a homophobic culture, a person could well be inclined to hate these feelings in some other who is or is perceived to be homosexual. Of course entire cultures and nations "project" this way too, the Nazi movement being just one terrible example.

So the phenomenon of projection points to the absolute necessity of dealing with one's own inner world, interacting with it in various ways, not just for the sake of mental and emotional health but for the sake of others and ultimately for the sake of the planet. Underlying this and other forms of human interaction is the phenomenon of consciousness. Perhaps some people make a decision to remain unconscious because their attempts at self-expression and self-definition have been damaged somehow.

Whatever the case, the seeking of maximum consciousness is the ideal, for without consciousness and self-awareness, projections become rampant to everyone's disadvantage. Which is not to say that all projecting is negative. Falling in love feels positive and that too is a projection. So we tend to project whatever is unconscious, both the positive and negative.

If a person can get in the habit of paying conscious attention to possible projections, as it were, catching and withdrawing them, then significant learning can take place. In this way people can "own" their projections and try to figure out what they mean rather than letting them remain unconscious and potentially problematic.

But how is one to know when projecting is taking place? One good way is to become conscious of when you are feeling strong emotions and at the same time feeling the urge to express them at someone else (individual or group), as though at a target. To get this kind of awareness can be very growth inducing in a person because it tells you what's "in there," and then you know more consciously what you have to deal with. Of course, it's easier to catch others in their projections, but to point that out might result in some explosive exchanges unless you are a confidant of the other and on very good terms.

Psychological Functions (Ego)

In Jungian and other systems, the number "Four" is considered a completion or wholeness number. So, for example, there are four psychological functions: two for perceiving: sensation and intuition, and two for deciding: thinking and feeling. This is not the place to go into this in detail, but each person lives out of some combination of these four functions and in a mostly extraverted or introverted way. Usually one function is dominant and one is weak. The weak function is a doorway to the personal shadow. If you don't know yourself in this regard, try to do some testing on it.

Jung wrote a book called Psychological Functions, which is somewhat difficult to read, but there's an interesting little book with a self-test called Please Understand Me by David Kiersey and Marilyn Bates that also has some practical applications of typology.

Understanding oneself in these ways and getting some grasp of the influence of extraversion and introversion on one's manner of perceiving and behaving can be very helpful both in inner and outer life. This is part of a Quantum approach since we are dealing here with forms of communication and relationship.

A commonly accepted shorthand in typology is: E = extraversion, I = introversion, S = sensation, N = intuition, T = thinking, F = feeling. The theory is that people usually have preferences in their basic stance toward things (E or I), each person usually has a preferential way of looking at reality (S or N), and deciding about what is being perceived (T or F), and each person also has a preference either for leaving things open-ended (P), or seeking closure (J).

Certain combinations of the functions yield four distinct personality types: SP (motivated by a need for "action"); SJ (motivated by a need for "belonging"); NT (motivated by a need for "exactness"); and, NF (motivated by a need to "search for meaning"). Interpersonal problems can often be traced to differences in Type.

In the Jungian schema, "extraversion" and "introversion" have to do with energy: the extravert finds energy in the outer world and the introvert in the inner world. Introverts tire easily if they have to pay too much attention to outer objects or persons, and extraverts become easily distracted and bored by introspection. It is difficult for an extravert to comprehend that for the introvert, inner life and objects can be more real and interesting than the outer world. In terms of the Quantum World, extraversion and introversion are closely connected to the most fundamental phenomena of moving toward (extraversion) and moving away from (introversion) and in persons these are the tendencies least likely to change very much.

Applying psychological functions to institutional life can be very illuminating. For example, some people are slow to be critical of church authority and of their congregations because for them institutions hold a high place in their value system (SJ). Some church members and ministers seem to always find projects to be engaged in (SP). Parishioners who tend to be very exacting in their expectations of preaching and teaching might well be NT's, and those in the forefront of liturgical and other ecclesial reform efforts will most likely be NF's.

Whatever field you work in or even in your own family, knowledge of these functions and of the tendencies underlying them can prove beneficial to positive engagement and relationship with others. Of course they don't explain everything about human behavior: there's more to us than psychological functions and some people have learned to adapt to situations which require them to act against their natural psychological tendencies (see Chapter 11).

All the above psychological functions and attitudes and all combinations of them, are archetypal. That means they can be very compulsive and unconscious. In the "J" attitude, for example, a person may feel simply forced to reach decisions. One experiences haste and panic. Getting to closure feels absolutely necessary, even though intellectually one might conclude there's really no rush. On the other hand, one with a "P" attitude may feel compelled to avoid closure at all costs. And all these functions and attitudes and combinations of them are archetypal. One would have to admit that quite frequently, we don't have them, they have us.

Heroes and Heroines

Another quaternity a person would do well to figure out and pay attention to is that of Mother/Father (Parent), Daughter/Son (Child), Warrior/Amazon (Hero), and Wise Man/Wise Woman (Senex). Again, each of us usually lives out of one of these archetypes primarily with its opposite being in the shadow and the other two more or less available. So, e.g., don't expect a parent type to be naturally inclined to egalitarian, wild, spontaneous adventures. And don't expect a Wise Person, studious type, to want to go off and join the Army.

Again, if you don't know which of these is your primary and which your shadow style and helper character, try to figure it out. This kind of knowledge, both of self and more significant others can be most helpful in relationships of all kinds and can help cut down on unnecessary misunderstandings. The Quantum point here is that people inevitably tend to feel, think and act out of these "typical" forms or archetypes so they color ways of being and consequently one's interactions and one's relationships.

Now, these archetypal forces are more general than the very specific ones popularized by Pearson and Corlett. They can be helpful in getting a general sense of where a person tends to be archetypally; then, eventually, one can look for more applicable specific archetypes.

Even the way a person is inclined to be "spiritual" comes out of type and character. Of course, these categories are not meant to define a person; people are too complicated to be defined, but they can help us understand ourselves and others better and give us some guidance in trying to understand how we "work."

Living in a community setting, provided it is truly a "community" and the members aren't exaggeratedly individualistic, helps a person gain some insight about one's strengths and weaknesses, talents, and lack of them, and wherein one can best contribute to the common good. So in this community-centered collaboration and sometimes clashing of egos, one learns humility or at least is forced to take a more realistic look at oneself. This interaction of archetypes (egos, in this case) is counter-cultural in that it happens not to see who wins, but in order to purify. It's a kind of alchemical process that stands in direct contrast to the will to power. What these "egos" are seeking is how to live in conformity with the will of God rather than their own wills.

Alchemy

Jung wrote extensively on several subjects. One of them was Alchemy. He concluded that many of the European alchemists, while purporting to be interested in transforming base matter into gold, were in actuality doing inner work of a psychological nature. He quotes an old alchemical notion: "Aurum nostrum non est aurum vulgi," which is Latin for "Our gold is not ordinary gold." So they were looking for a sort of inner "gold" or what Jesus refers to as "the inner Reign of God." Alchemy eventually branched into Chemistry on the one hand, and Depth Psychology on the other.

Alchemy is quite complicated in its descriptions of procedures and processes, but in general it refers to the human experience of at times falling apart, reorganizing one's life and then getting oneself more or less back together again for a while, only to have the process repeated again, hopefully with progressively better outcomes. In this sense, the labyrinth is an alchemical symbol, as is the "aurobourus," the snake eating its own tail: both are circular, spiral symbols indicating movement toward and away from the Center (Self). And the individuation process described metaphorically in alchemy, often requires at many points along the way, that a person pay close attention to what is lacking: "opus contra naturam" (described in chapter 11).

The Ego-Self Axis

In Jungian terms, the Ego (initially as Innocent), experiences alienation from the Self and then eventually experiences a healing of that rift as though by grace (Transcendent Function). Some Jungian authors describe this as an Ego-Self Axis: that inevitably a person's Ego separates so far from the nature of the Self that a split occurs, something akin to what Christian theology calls original sin. The "call" then is to seek a healing in that split which one can work at in various ways, both inner (psychological work, such as with dreams and fantasies), and outer (altruistic work such as on behalf of justice, ecology, feminism, etc.). An old Taoist proverb says: "The way in is the way out." The actual ultimate experience of healing (a sort of salvation and redemption), is felt as grace. To take credit for such an experience would lead a person to Ego-inflation, which would bring about even more alienation.

Many people report mystical, deeply spiritual experiences, especially after undergoing long periods of suffering of some kind. These experiences are felt as moving a person toward union with the divine in some way and they stay alive in memory as a moment of grace and illumination. Archetypaly, this is an experience of the Self. It is resurrection after crucifixion in a Christian theological way of viewing things.

Narcissism

Again, interaction is the basic unit of psychological life. This interaction is most fundamentally an interaction of archetypes and their fields. That inner conversation can be distorted in various ways. One of them is through what is called "narcissism." Remember the Greek god Narcissus, who fell in love with his own reflection in a pool of water? He became so enamored of himself that he turned solid there sitting by the pond, utterly oblivious to the rest of life. All people are narcissistic to some extent. That just means a healthy self-interest and concern for one's own well being. But too much of this results in preoccupation with oneself to the detriment of relating with others or even in having interest in the outer world except insofar as such interest redounds to oneself.

No doubt most of us at times come up against people who either cannot or will not make allowances for others. They just forge ahead with their own agendas and ideologies oblivious to what other people around them might be thinking, intending or feeling. This is a form of narcissism. It would be quite logical to suppose that a path of healing for such narcissism lies in accepting reality as intrinsically interactive and trying to live accordingly.

In terms of narcissism, the person so afflicted would be too identified with his or her own ego. In this sense, there's a natural narcissism in the very young without which they wouldn't be able to make their needs known and so wouldn't be able to survive. But as one matures, narcissistic behavior needs to be left behind and other people and outer events taken more into account.

Born Again

Christian theology speaks of the experience of the Holy Spirit: alienation and disruptions of various kinds occur in someone's life and then, eventually, a re-birth happens. For most people this is a repetitive process. Another way of describing this is by way of Dante's Divine Comedy: from hell and purgatory up to heaven; from Cross to Resurrection. A way of speaking about this experience that is more religiously "neutral" is to use the term "soul-making." I understand this expression to mean that people are born and exist intrinsically as spiritual beings, but that it takes work to turn spirit into soul. And that "opus" (alchemy again), takes place primarily through relationships. People know and can to some extent speak about their moments of soulfulness. One of the books I list in this paper (and previously mentioned in the text), as suggested reading is titled, Death of the Hero, Birth of the Soul. The implication in the title is that (this is a book specifically for men), at a certain time in life, the call is for a man to stop trying so hard, to lay aside the heroics and the competition and develop some soul (more of the feeling function, joy in living, less stress, less work, more play, less Warrior and more Lover).

Synchronicity http://en.wikipedia.org/wiki/Synchronicity

With some frequency people use the expression, "What a coincidence!" Maybe it's a coincidence and maybe it's "synchronicity." This word refers to the experience of something happening outside a person that mysteriously corresponds to something going on within. For instance: a young man goes out to start up his car and the battery is dead. Just before he went outside he mentioned to a friend on the phone, "Boy, my batteries are sure low today; I feel drained." That would be an experience of synchronicity.

For someone who sees reality through Quantum lenses, synchronicity wouldn't seem unusual. In fact such a person would perhaps get in the habit of looking for such events as the norm, since, after all, everything is connected as one gigantic web and what is present in one place on the web is somehow present everywhere. One could classify "resonance" as a kind of synchronicity. Resonance means that people are finding their personal vibrations matching; there's a mutual attraction and a felt sense of living in a shared reality. The book listed in the Bibliography by Penny Peirce, Frequency: the Power of Personal Vibration, offers many wonderful insights into this experience.

A Dream

I'm on the reservation. People are milling around quietly and things seem very peaceful. One of the ladies there has covered herself completely in her blanket. She begins to wail in the old language used to mourn the dead. The more she wails the more others join in. People begin to dance also swaying in tune to the chanting. I go up close to the lady and try to get my voice to match hers in intensity. Slowly she begins to quiet down. She uncovers her head, I look at her, and she begins to laugh. She is now very peaceful and happy.

Notice I underline concrete objects of the dream. That's because, were I to want to interpret the dream, I would look first for the intrinsic meanings of the objects, what they symbolize.

I used to go on Sundays and for funeral Masses to a reservation near San Diego called "Viejas." I once attended a wake for a relatively young man who had died unexpectedly. The tribe does have its own language, though it's not much in use on the U.S. side of the border. The tribal group also has villages in Baja California and by law the members may freely move back and forth for tribal business and family relationships. The name of the tribe and language is "Kumeyaay." Apart from the tribal language, the group maintains and passes down orally another language that is only used for mourning the dead. I've heard it might be related to Yuma language. Anyway, the people chant this language at their wakes and the sound, with its mournful, wailing notes, seems geared to produce sadness and grief in the hearers and the singers.

I wonder what this dream is trying to tell me? I think very much like other dreams I have included in this paper: look for what resonates; trust the non-rational more; have regard for your "persona" but in situations of resonance and trust, let it soften (remove the blanket). However, as with most dreams, there's more to it than that. Also, dreams want to be worked with, over and over, and I'll certainly be working more with this one! Note too, that dreams will make use of our own experiences to teach us something important we need to learn even if the learning is of a different sort than the original experience.

Images, the collective unconscious and grace

Most therapies work just with the personal unconscious. Jung emphasized the collective unconscious. The collective unconscious is also a center of attention in the Assisi approach. The work from this perspective is not about interpretation but *translation.* So one takes an image and its context and "translates" it. Another word for this is "orientation." (see Ulanov, 2004, p. 29). We are trying to understand the innate nature of something. Forget subjective views; what does the image mean? Learn the language of whatever image you're looking at. You might have to do some research. Like, the image of a gas gauge not working in a car. What does this image say? You don't know if you have enough "gas" to get you to where you want to go. Often an image will tell you about whatever process an individual is involved in. It might be about how the therapy is going too. The image poses questions about how much energy one has for something (this imagery is from a Conforti seminar).

I believe it is one's ability and propensity to live in and act out of the Quantum side of things which gives one the capacity to have insights into the collective unconscious and to be able to perceive fields, patterns and archetypes. And, again, it's a good idea to be aware that not all people feel inclined to get into this Quantum perspective and that many people even find this world repugnant or too mystical to pay attention to. Perhaps there's nothing quite as basic causing tension and conflict between people than this: that some can move with ease and comfort in and out of a Quantum way of perceiving, and others feel quite caught in the world of explicate reality, imprisoned as it were in a Newtonian world. I imagine that explains why in any despotic regime the most suspect segment of the population are the artists and poets since their inspirations and insights are a threat to more literal-minded and regimented people.

Both Augustine and Jung demonstrate this facility to move in and out of the Quantum world. Augustine, though, seems more integrated and less inclined to compartmentalize. Jung, maybe more as a reaction to his critics than from conviction, shys away from the metaphysical and theological. For Augustine, reality is one. And reality is imbued with grace.

There's an underlying quest in this paper to get at the most underlying and most fundamental realities underlying things, and the conclusion is that this is the world of the archetypes and the world of the Quantum. But were one to enquire of St. Augustine what he might think of all this, I imagine he'd say that the most fundamental reality of all is the divine and divine grace at work everywhere, that somehow or other we all have being and move about buoyed up by the powerful yet subtle flow of grace: it precedes us, accompanies us and awaits us. To claim power for oneself is to miss the mark. But "we can do all things in he who strengthens us." Whether or not Carl Jung would have agreed with the above, I don't know. But I think he would have preferred to keep his own counsel on the matter, due to having been criticized about not being sufficiently scientific.

In terms of living in community and psychologically, emotionally and spiritually rubbing up against one another, hopefully little by little people can come to realize if their strengths lie more on the Newtonian or Quantum side of things and employ their talents accordingly. The more consciousness of this the better, not just so one can avoid a job or ministry placement that doesn't fit well, but even more importantly, so one can find that "place" wherein flowering can take place. In this sense a community, with whatever diversity is there, can be helpful in helping its members discern what Self (God) seems to be calling them to. They can voice their concerns and observations to each other and to those who traditionally are most concerned with discernment and ministry assignments. I hope the reader can "see" how the archetypes of ego, Self, shadow, psychological functions and many others, are bubbling around in us and between us, and how our consciousness of their activity is so important.

Animus/Anima

Of all the archetypes of the human psyche I find this one the most difficult to theorize about and comprehend. The Ulanovs in their many books and especially in Transforming Sexuality, offer some clear explanations of this archetype and its workings. These so-called contra-sexual energy systems, usually personified as persons of the opposite sex to one's own, are guides to relationship: specifically to relationship with one's own Self internally, and to relating with other people. As I read their descriptions, I feel led to think that being with people someone feels attracted to, being in relationship with them, is, in fact, being in relationship with images of one's Self, and that these friendships or other forms of relating are ultimately helpful in establishing or reestablishing connection to the Self.

I also feel led to believe that it's best not to insist too much on a need for opposite sex images for one's anima or animus. I think, rather, that this archetypal energy system will take on and so manifest itself symbolically in both male and female forms depending on which one specifically best incorporates what's missing from consciousness. I imagine that usually a male's anima will image as feminine and a female's animus as masculine, but not always. And a more feminine male's anima may well appear in dreams or in some outer figure as a masculine woman, and a more masculine female's animus as a feminine male, and, of course, at times too as same sex images. The basic consideration here is that the contra sexual archetypal symbols and images are complementary to that which has been consciously developed.

As one can hopefully appreciate, anima/animus incarnations are not terribly neat and predictive. But relating with them consciously is very crucial because in relating they will lead one to the Self.

In the preceding sections I have presented some thoughts on important aspects of several fields of human experience and study. In this section I specifically zero in on the contra sexual archetypes of the human psyche, Animus (the Other of the human female) and Anima (the Other of the human male). As in the preceding, I hope to offer descriptions that are clear and understandable even if I run the risk of being too simplistic. Getting as clear as possible a grasp of the contra-sexual archetypes is, I think, the key to understanding Jungian depth psychology. And without this understanding one is unable to grasp the complications of what is meant by Self.

The general aim of Jungian depth psychology (Analytical Psychology) is "wholeness." So one is trying to get consciousness (ego) to become as aware as possible of whatever is in the "unconscious." In the dialogical process called analysis, and in inner work done personally apart from a formal analysis, the client will hopefully so relate with the unconscious, both personal and collective, that all the different complexes and their archetypes will get untangled and differentiated, not dominating or flooding or possessing ego, and not being dominated, flooded or possessed by ego either. In an Augustinian community setting wherein, hopefully, the members are dedicated to assisting each other to grow as people in grace (so quantum-wise, holistically), the members will be concerned that there be a balance collectively between masculine and feminine energy. Also in each one usually a person can determine from self-awareness if there is a good balance, or if there is too much of one energy system at the expense of the other. What an individual and a community are ultimately looking toward is "individuation." And that means a good balance of all the psychic energy systems; and the archetypes are the nuclei of all psychic energy systems.

The ultimate goal of Jungian analysis is individuation and the inner marriage (the sacred matrimony to which all are called) of masculine and feminine (ego & anima/animus). Dream work and active imagination lead one in the direction of individuation. In Christian terms: union of the soul with Christ.

The ultimate goal of Christian spirituality is union with God (described also as union with Christ). The sacraments and a life of prayer, study and action for justice, lead one in this direction. Thus religion and psychology (with its call to do inner work) though different, are very similar in their goals.

As one deals with parental complexes, one is confronting and re-shaping Persona. As one deals with the "enemy" both within and without, one is confronting and coming to understandings with Shadow. As one deals with those within and without toward whom one feels attraction and affection, one is cultivating Anima/Animus. And this latter bridges us to the Self.

And at some point or points when Self (God) is ready, the transcendent function (Holy Spirit) will come and heal the Ego-Self connection. This is experienced as happening as though by grace.

Animus/Anima create a bridge between ego and self and also a bridge to the world "out there." The "Contra-sexual" archetype is understood in a psychological sense, not necessarily biological; thus a masculine anima or feminine animus. Check your projections if you want to identify what your particular anima or animus are like: what kind of people are you attracted to?

So the work of the contra-sexual archetype is to lead ego to Self. One can consciously work at this by thinking about and being with those people for whom one feels attraction since that attraction indicates that they are outer images reflective of Animus or Anima. Their presence to one is healing, i.e., it helps reconnect ego to Self. This inner work also then prepares one for the coming of the transcendent function that is even more healing.

This archetypal, "contra sexual" (the other) energy called anima/animus gets constellated as a complement to whatever one's conscious, manifest sexual energy is like. This can be less than neat: doesn't one's manifest, conscious way of being a sexual person fluctuate? So wouldn't the so-called contra sexual archetype and its images fluctuate too? And this might explain why it is that one moment this person attracts you, the next moment someone else, and as you change, so do the objects of your projections, which, of course, are giving you hints about the nature of your anima/animus.

Animus/Anima serve as inner guides, leading the ego toward self. They are also outer guides, in that their energy gives a person strength and ability to relate with others. One can see a connection between being connected with Self and feeling connected with others. (How can you love God whom you don't see, unless you love people whom you do)

Archetypes: concentrations or constellations of energy around some feeling-charged theme. With animus/anima, the energy constellated includes that of an individual's unconscious and undeveloped sexuality (the Other). Complexes are personalized archetypes, a shell around a central core or nucleus of some archetype.

In others and ourselves we don't deal with archetypes as such which are pure potency for some gathering of energy, but with complexes, i.e., a given person's way of incarnating and living out some archetype.

Complexes can be more or less healthy, or they may be problematic if not sufficiently integrated by the ego and even a cause of neurosis. How can someone get a grip on some negative complex and do something about it?

If you know yourself well or some other(s) know you well, you or they might be able to discern from certain behaviors that you are in the grip of some complex: such as a notable change in personality, some compulsive behavior, irritability or mood swings.

In order to emerge from some complex or addiction and be able to gain control over the compulsions behind it, a person needs to be in relationship with the divine as she or he understands that, and to do what one can to prepare for such a relationship, one has to admit powerlessness over the complex or addiction or whatever the particular challenge is, confess oneself to a person of confidence, and turn one's life over to a transcendent higher power (the divine) as one understands and imagines that.

4

A NEW PARADIGM

It is my intent in this chapter to demonstrate how our paradigms come out of the physical sciences and how changes in these sciences necessitate changes in our paradigms. I introduce here some concepts on the relational nature of divinity from a Christian perspective and I define what is meant by the "holon" as the central metaphor of the new paradigm. I then briefly indicate how this new paradigm provides us with a unified theory that takes in all of reality. I allude to a religious problem: that of reconciling one's own belief system, specifically one's sacred texts, with this new paradigm. Finally, I describe what I consider to be the core or nucleus of the new paradigm in behavioral terms. I highlight that part because it's something to keep always in mind and is at least somewhat concrete and specific.

Now we will deal with the physical world. People get their paradigms or ways of organizing their thoughts about reality, principally from the so-called "hard" sciences. The trouble is that there's paradigm confusion. Maybe some of your co-religionists are still acting out of a belief in a cosmology more appropriate to second century Greco-Roman culture, a cosmology (Ptolemaic) believed in by the authors of the Hebrew and Christian scriptures, but long since discredited. Needless to say, if *you* hold to a more modern, evolution-embracing cosmology, you will find it difficult to discuss important issues with them (your co-religionists).

Both the Quantum and the traditional Newtonian approaches to physical reality (in some combination) are going to provide a new paradigm or are already providing it. And of great interest to me in seeking a unified theory is that in both cases, whether one is describing planets, galaxies or entire universes, or the inner-most workings of atoms, the most basic reality of material existence is again "interaction" or (perhaps a better word), relationship, and the fields interpenetrating and containing them.

The One and the Many

Theology is the study of God. Ultimately, God is the most basic relationship of love, both within and without. I'm not sure how this notion of the Divine as somehow "community" would go over in Jewish and Islamic circles because of their great emphasis on the unitary nature of God. I think at least the subject can be broached starting from the doctrine of God as One that is also shared by the Christian churches.

From there such a dialogue might address the issue of "linguistics" in the sense that Persons as used in Greek at the early Church Councils referred to "masks" or manifested personalities rather than persons as understood in modern Western languages. This line of thinking leads to this consideration: do some theologies over- emphasize God's oneness and others over- emphasize God's inner diversity?

In Christian theology the Father is in intimate relationship and interaction with the Son and both with the Spirit. Since there are trinity concepts of divinity in other religions as well (e.g., Hinduism), this could be a fruitful place for inter-religious understanding. (In a psychological way, each human person is a trinity of Self, Ego and Transcendent Function).

Were we to begin our musings on this subject with God (which is what traditional theology does: it starts with what is believed to be a revelation of some kind and as this revelation is described in scripture), it would be most reasonable to assume from the outset that all of creation, and people specifically, would have this same characteristic of interaction/relationship as their basic reality since they are made in God's image. One might also argue on this basis of the need people have for "community."

The Holon

Jesus tells us that God is love. That would lead us to believe that when people are living at their best in terms of interaction, that they're living lovingly. That tells us that where there is lack of love: unjust discrimination and prejudices of various kinds, skapegoating, hateful words and actions, etc., that such people are not in touch with their humanity.

The central metaphor that Quantum Theology uses (this theology is inductive, starting with human experiences of all possible kinds, seeking the divine phenomenologically) is the "Holon." This metaphor is from quantum physics: every entity which is somehow complete in itself is nonetheless part of some greater whole and reflective of it (the whole is always greater than the sum of its parts) and every whole can be further broken down into "wholes" which reflect the greater whole (or, reality tends to be "fractal" in many different ways).

There is, then, a basic underlying whole through which all things are related. We are moving toward some understanding of all of reality in this metaphor. If you want to go more into this concept, check out what the scientist David Bohme means when he uses the terms "implicate" and "explicate" orders (pp. 56 & 57 in Quantum Theology by Diarmuid O'Murchu). I see the basic, underlying reality of this "holon" view, that which is present in all areas of life, as interaction/relationship/archetypes. Other aspects of the Holon are "shadow" (darkness), light, chaos, and fields.

47

This is Our Story

You can also take some Jungian insights about the inner world and theologize on them, coming up, for example with the suggestion that we are all also the characters of Scripture: i.e., that if you want to make your religion come alive phenomenologically, enter into the stories: speak with the characters in active imagination; realize that they also live in you and are part of you; give them their due and give them voice. What one is dealing with is the world of archetypes, even in the symbolism and imagery of scripture. That makes the scriptures come alive and also adds much to religious celebrations. When I do this in homilies, I can see the congregation come alive and really be present. I've seen the opposite, too!

To summarize: God is most basically a community of loving interaction. The most basic unit of human group life is interaction. The most basic unit of psychological life is interaction. The most basic component of physical reality large and small is relationship. And all these interactions involve the interplay either of archetypes or sub-atomic particles or both (probably the latter is most accurate).

A Unified Theory

Are you looking for a unified theory? This is the one that makes most sense to me. It combines the best insights of sociology, psychology, physics and theology. It provides a tool for evaluation as well since what one would ask about the health of one's social group, one's psyche/soul and the world at large, is: how are the interactions? What is the quality of our relationships? What can we do to improve them? What stands in the way? What can we do about the ozone layer so as to restore some ecological balance? It seems to me that this is the area we must really pay close attention to (I mean relationships of all kinds). And we need to pay attention to all of them simultaneously. Which means that we need to pay very close and very conscious attention to our own and others' archetypes since that's the very "stuff" of interaction/relationship.

In some areas of the world, people build their homes using adobe bricks. They prepare some adobe mud, mix in straw and sometimes other substances, and then put the adobe into frames until it sufficiently hardens. The wooden frame or mold is like an archetype. When it's just "there," it's empty. But then some archetype gets constellated in a particular person or group, and it fills up with that person or group's stuff. Then you may have some "complex" which has colored the archetype. So the archetype as such is pure potency until it incarnates in a person or group and so gets actualized.

Not all archetypes become complexes. Some may, but others stay as "pure" archetypes simply influencing the individual toward certain kinds of thinking, feeling and behavior. And even those archetypes that do become complexes don't necessarily become too problematic provided one can become conscious of them. Then they can even help construct the real if complicated personality of the person.

How do people get in touch with their archetypes, especially the more influential and/or problematic ones? Sometimes others become aware of people's complexes before the individuals themselves, and they point out that there might be a problem. And how do they become aware of the complex? Perhaps through behavior seen as unusual for the person. Or, another picks up on some field and deduces the presence of some complex behind the field. Or a dream might reveal an archetype or a complex. And, if a person is quite conscious and introspective, he or she might conclude the presence of a problematic archetype and complex as they catch themselves in a projection and come to awareness about the nature of the projection.

Paradigm Shift

The scriptures of the various world religions were all composed several centuries ago. They are to one degree or another held as sacred and divinely inspired by their adherents and in some cases ought not even be translated into modern languages since it is believed that God dictated them in a particular sacred tongue. Inevitably the accepted scientific view of the time of writing forms part of the text. One major challenge for all believers of any religion is to continue to hold to their religious system while acknowledging the errors of the scientific views found in the religion's sacred texts.

Whenever a society, such as ours, comes up with a whole new scientific explanation of things, then people have to articulate a new paradigm or world-view. So religious metaphors remain true but come to be in need of new mediums to carry them afresh into the future. This is the job of a paradigm. One thesis of this paper is that there is such an emerging paradigm that can be referred to as Quantum Theology.

Another way to speak of this paradigm shift is to use the word "relativity." My understanding as this is used metaphorically in the social sciences and in theology (though it doesn't mean this in Einstein's theories), is that objectivity is very hard to come by. Not that there's no objectivity, only that there's less than we used to think. And to get toward objectivity, people need to be in rather continual interchange with others around important issues. What is basically objective is the interaction/relationship underlying all of reality, and the archetypes and fields involved in those interactions.

In a concrete kind of way, this new paradigm notion includes the inclination to be simultaneously looking at four levels of reality and seeing their fractal nature and deducing from that some metaphors. The four levels are: outer and deep space (the Multiverse), inner space (as in sub-atomic entities), psychic space (esp. as described in analytical psychology), and organizational space. As I do that kind of exercise myself I am led to wonder about the similarities between dark matter and energy and the shadow, between complexes and black holes, between the faces of organizations and the ways people have of organizing their personas. Even to wondering about how we tend sometimes to think of our own earth and galaxy as so terribly important (while in the bigger picture of billions of galaxies and even of maybe billions of universes making up the multiverse), it's not so crucial. And then to see *that* as fractal to the human inclination to exaggerate one's ego and get all inflated when really the ego is very small and insignificant compared to the Self and its centrality in the psyche. And that the ego of any given organization might be inclined to do the same thing.

I find this kind of exercise enlightening and that on many levels it contributes to a felt sense that somehow all reality is connected as though in some strange gigantic vibrating web of which we are all a part.

Archetypes fit into this quantum worldview because they are common to all people in their essential inner core. Individuals experience the archetypes differently because their own personal histories with any particular archetype form a kind of "crust" around it and so particularize it. Also, the archetypes behave in an individual much like sub-atomic entities, as fairly unpredictable and indeterminate, and "not holding still" when someone tries to examine them. And we live in two worlds at once: one the Newtonian world of predictability and measurement, the other, the Quantum world of indeterminacy and unpredictability. Each person is more at home in one of these worlds than in the other, but we all are called upon to learn to live in both. Usually any particular situation is requesting either a Newtonian or a Quantum response. Sometimes people will misread the exigencies of situations and respond inappropriately; for example, looking for precision and predictability in a Quantum situation or presuming unpredictability in a Newtonian situation. I had a theology professor who would say things like "There are three persons in the Trinity, more or less." But maybe he was seeing something Quantum in what wanted to pass for a Newtonian world.

Here's an interesting observation by Buckminster Fuller: "In order to change an existing paradigm you do not struggle to try and change the problematic model. You create a new model and make the old one obsolete." I got the quote second-hand from Penny Peirce, 2009, p. 185, and she doesn't say where he wrote or spoke that, but I find it to be very accurate and very consoling. It also makes me think that we do already have "new models": religious orders, esp. the democratic ones, the Sufi orders in Islam, and other basically egalitarian and peace promoting groups. I think Augustine would agree with Mr. Fuller too and he'd probably suggest that one would do well to wait on God's grace and real substantial inspiration before tinkering with a paradigm that probably won't respond well to direct pushing.

The core or nucleus of the new paradigm

It's clarifying for me once in a while to concentrate on the outcomes I'd like to see in people and organizations once they're familiar with the content of this new paradigm and have decided to use it as a kind of guiding methodology. So what I'd be hoping for is that such people would have a good grasp of how reality is both predictable and measurable, (yang and Newtonian), and unpredictable, yin and Quantum), and that they would see how it's really necessary to move between both these worlds and decide when one is more appropriate than the other. And I'd want to see such people concretely checking themselves out on the basis of Jung's map of the soul: how am I doing in terms of persona and shadow issues as I feel them impact me? Am I trying to become more conscious of the contents of the unconscious? Am I sensing that my identity, my ego, is pretty much in tune with my self (the inner God-principle) or am I tending more in the direction of alienation from the way I'm meant to be? Am I experiencing a fairly good balance of yin and yang energy, of the masculine and feminine, or is there too much of an imbalance in my system? What are my dreams telling me about myself, as well my illnesses and my bodily and emotional state, and my projections? Am I aware of my stronger psychological functions and at the same time am I trying to develop those functions that, being in the shadow and so unconscious, tend to trip me up? Am I enough aware of my stronger developmental archetypes (see especially Chapter 11, Opus Contra Naturam), and at the same time trying to be in touch with my under-developed ones?

Now one would take the above paragraph and also apply the concepts to one's groups and institutions. Of course in doing that, you'd have to identify the ego of the group and go through all the above speculation getting the group ego to respond. And eventually, after much discussion, the group ego might want to suggest some ways to move the group or organization toward greater wholeness and so effectiveness.

All the above has to do with trying to get consciousness to become ever more conscious and this would include being willing to engage with the unconscious, even if this means a kind of confrontation. In engaging in this task of living according to a new paradigm, individuals might want to be accompanied by a guide of some kind, or a soul mate, or a therapist or psychoanalyst or minister. And organizations would do well to seek the accompaniment of an organizational consultant with an interest and hopefully a background in this kind of holistic organizational analysis.

Now, while doing all the things I just alluded to, one who is interested in living according to this model I call a new paradigm would also be a person of deep prayer, and, with some frequency admitting powerlessness in the face of addictions and other seemingly insurmountable problems as they surface. This is not a way to repress or suppress what needs to be looked at. It is simply a kind of spirituality (Augustinian) that admits that one is not all-powerful but rather very dependent on the divine both within and without and most needful also of humility. From an Augustinian perspective, one is thus avoiding falling into the extremes represented historically by Pelagius (too much dependence on oneself and one's own consciousness), and Donatus (we have to be perfect or at least seem to be perfect and without sin). Another very Augustinian notion is that the human quest for the divine really needs the context of community for it to remain healthy. Not only are we absolutely dependent upon God for existence and for grace; we are also dependent upon one another. Augustine (and many other people too), mostly experience the divine at work through the mediation of others. For Augustine, the community of friends is what brought him out of the morass of the Manicheans into the intellectual enlightenment of the Neo-Platonic Philosophers and finally into his true home, Catholic Christianity.

See esp. for the above: *Corlett, John G. & Carol S. Pearson, <u>Mapping the Organizational Psyche: A Jungian Theory of Organizational Dynamics and Change</u>, Gainesville, FL, 2003.

The Dominant of this study: summaries of theories of the social, psychological, theological and quantum sciences, especially concentrating on archetypal field theory and Augustinian spirituality and their connection with Quantum thought, are presented, with a view toward articulating a holistic view of reality and the pressing need to move toward more collaborative ways of being.

(I repeat the Dominant of this study with some frequency as a way to keep focused).

5

EDUCATION

As in the other chapters, I am concerned here mainly with showing the natural centrality of interaction and relationship together with certain archetypes. I do that by describing the educational approaches of Paulo Freire and Carl Rogers as well as my own attempts at educational praxis and theory. Some other applications of educational interaction I go into in this chapter are those of psychotherapy and family counseling.

Freire

One specific application of this unified theory is in education. Some years ago, in the mid sixties, a Brazilian educator, Paulo Freire, wrote a book entitled Pedagogy of the Oppressed. He summarizes his educational practice and theory in that book as consisting primarily of "dialogue": i.e., the teacher who is also always a student (archetype of Everyperson), engages the students who are always also teachers (Ruler and Sage archetypes), in dialogical interaction around emotionally-charged themes from their lived experience. In this context they learn to think critically and reflectively and to read and write at the same time. As I remember my own educational experiences both as student and as teacher, that rings true. I explicitly used Freire's methodology in teaching "campesinos" biblical literacy in Peru (1972-1975) and I try to be as interactive as possible in any educational work in which I engage.

Dialogue is the method Freire suggests for teaching oppressed people. Dialogue requires the active participation of the students, and it requires the teacher to allow the students' ideas to become part of the discussion, instead of directing the discussion to something the teacher wants to say. BookRags (2011-10-25). Pedagogy of the Oppressed by Paulo Freire, Summary & Study Guide (Kindle Locations 155-157). Kindle Edition.

People appreciate having their thoughts taken into account and learn better in the give and take of dialogue. In fact, lack of ability to engage with another dialogically can be terribly frustrating and destructive of community. Personally, I'd much rather be with people and interact with people who are dialogical whatever their religious background than with members of my own faith or cultural tradition who are not.

This is not to imply that Freire's approach should be uncritically accepted. There are some problems connected with educating people in liberation thought (as in Brazil in

1966) in very dangerous situations where they are not going to be protected by law or the courts. In this sense one must proceed very prudently and not put others at unnecessary risk under the guise of education. And yet what good is any education if it is not in some way liberating?

Part of Freire's liberating education emphasizes that it is very easy and very common for an oppressed person to become an oppressor.

Rogers

I was a member of a psychological institute in La Jolla (Center For Studies of the Person) for a few years (1979-1981). During a weekly meeting, I mentioned the educational method of Freire to the psychologist Carl Rogers, the founder of the institute. He responded that it sounded very much like his own therapeutic theory wherein the therapist engages a client by being empathic (entering the world of the other), unconditionally accepting, and appropriately revelatory. What we have in both these approaches (Freire and Rogers) is the centrality of interaction/relationship, and I believe (though neither Freire nor Rogers were proponents of archetypal theory), that their methods do indeed stir up the archetypes, sometimes very powerfully, such as the Warrior, the Caregiver, the Seeker and the Creator.

My own critique of Rogers and his method would be that it's too laissez-faire and that sometimes the more dominant types take over and engage in bullying tactics. As a psychotherapeutic tool I believe it works well for a time. At some point, it seems to me, it's more appropriate to be somewhat directive and content-centered, as with dreams and the archetypes that get surfaced.

There are differences of technique, however. Freire's method presumes an activist, interventionist instructor who continually keeps the participants off-balance and intense. In Rogers' method, there might be a facilitator, but that person takes a rather passive role and operates out of a conviction that the person or group must discover its own path and take responsibility for its own direction. So these are very different methodologies though having in common an emphasis on relationship.

Rogers was of the view that psychotherapy and education are so intimately linked that what was most essential to one would be true of the other. I think he was right to a certain extent and I believe he and Freire were on the same track through their emphasis on an interactive relationship.

Personal Reflections

My own experience in teaching and learning leads me to the conviction that the lecture style of imparting knowledge needs to be somehow interactive. I am aware that for various reasons, many (maybe most), people prefer this method (the lecture) both as students and as teachers. This may come across as rather jaded, but I think that's because the student can then take a fairly passive role and not fear becoming engaged in the learning process, and the instructor can preside unchallenged. Which is not to say that lectures are not sometimes interesting. I need to admit that there might be some people who do learn well from the lecture method. I certainly am not usually one of them. And part of my reflecting on this leads me to the conclusion that the lecture method does not usually help awaken any positive archetypes in me unless it is very engaging and pictorial. A little caveat: a good, well-prepared lecturer who loves his or her subject matter, can, nevertheless, be quite engaging.

The best learning I've been involved in both as teacher and learner has happened when the participants were unaware that learning was going on. For example, when other students had the role of leading a discussion and the instructor could then inject some ideas at appropriate moments and take the students unaware, as it were, before they had a chance to put up defenses or go off daydreaming. I also experience learning taking place when a sort of give and take gets going in an educational setting. The instructor would have some specific objectives in mind for a particular session and might even at some point communicate those objectives. These would serve the function of helping all present keep focused.

Again, for learning to take place, the instructor needs to concentrate not just on some content, but on engaging the students knowing that people are inclined to be passive unless their attention and interest is tapped. Some visuals, such as videos and power-point presentations, are also helpful in learning, but are best used not for entertainment purposes but rather as stimulators to get the participants to engage the material, really chew on it and become creative with it. In fact, if learning is going on in some setting, the Creator archetype is at work, and often also the Destroyer (letting a person know what attitudes and ways of acting need to be left behind as new ways [Creator] are taken on).

My own educational preference is to be involved in the religious education of adults. In that field one doesn't have to be much concerned about attendance or grades or testing or such things (Newtonian world). The downside is that you never really know who or how many might show up for some event, unless it's a formal course or has some reward attached to it.

Psychotherapy

Psychological and other forms of counseling (except for psychiatry which is largely medication-based) are educational by nature. Learnings take place both inductively and deductively. And, sometimes, basic shifts happen as when a person comes to realize and name certain felt problems or pathologies and accepts the fact that only he or she can do something about them (Orphan). Some people refer to this sort of counseling psychotherapy as the "talking cure." And, indeed, there is a great deal of talk involved in psychotherapy. Hopefully what happens in the exchanges between client and therapist, among other things, is the realization, "I can say anything and reveal anything to this person and I won't be judged or criticized for it."

Sometimes in a counseling situation, both therapist and client feel so caught up in subjectivity that they have a difficult time determining "what is wanted" in an objective sense. And that's the value of dreams and fantasies because even though they feel subjective and personal in nature, they speak out of an objective frame of reference and let a person know, mostly through metaphor, which ways to go and what needs to be done. Often the key archetypes at play in a client's life can be accessed from dream material.

Therapeutic healing doesn't necessarily mean that one's difficulties go away, but that one is better able to live with them, to include them in oneself, to enter into a conversation with them, and to own them as part of oneself. So a person discovers that the major block to recovery has been refusal to look at one's shadow and befriend it rather than such "symptoms" as depression, anxiety or borderline issues. The most basic reality in psychotherapy is relationship, both that between therapist and client and within each. And because of this relationship dimension, psychotherapy is included within a discussion of the New Paradigm. And, again, the most basic content of these interactions is archetypes.

Often, once a person has identified a dominant archetypal field, it may become clear that the field is also present in and operating through his or her own psyche. In a practical way, do I really want to move toward liberation and autonomy or do I prefer to stay dependent and just conform to accepted standards? An aspect of not seeking integral liberation as a person is manifested in people-pleasing behavior. In a liberation vs. patron context, this behavior leads to value and identity confusion and a person may become infected with extraneous "stuff" from people with stronger ego structures. These tendencies are for the most part unconscious but can be uncovered in psychotherapy and other forms of counseling.

Family Counseling

Since people are by nature relational beings, our psychological and emotional problems are often intertwined with those of others. This is especially true in families and this fact makes one question the ultimate value of individual psychotherapy. Whatever the case on that, there are situations in which the only reasonable course of action is involving the entire family in a group counseling situation, presuming, of course, a basic willingness on their part.

A few ground rules would be necessary at the outset in this kind of interaction: the participants agree not to engage in physical or verbal abuse, they express anger verbally as reflecting their own feelings and with some restraint and they agree about the distinction between perception and reality. For example, a family member might have had the experience of being a scapegoat yet that's not the perception of someone else in the family. Or a member expresses the feeling of having been neglected and that takes some other members by surprise. Another ground rule, expressly stated, would be that truth is to be sought wherever reflection might lead and that silence as a response can be deadly: any feelings of "don't talk, don't ask, don't tell" should be expressed and dealt with as obstacles to therapy. In the example of a family I mentioned previously as seeking therapy together, the above criteria would be very important and would need to be expressly stated and agreed to prior to beginning therapy.

What are the disciplines so far mentioned wherein relationship and archetypes hold such a central place? Sociology and Social Psychology, Clinical Psychology, Physics (both Newtonian and Quantum), Ecology, Education, Communication Theory, Theology and Psychological Counseling.

A Dream

A new school is being built near the Navy pier in San Diego, and on land that is now a parking lot, across from what used to be a building housing offices of the Navy. My mother worked there while I was in high school. The parking lot used to be Padre Field, home of the San Diego baseball team. I am told that I was selected to be one of the top administrators of the new school. My sense is that it is a high school.

Since this new school is being built near the bay, I would want to figure out what this symbolizes, as well as a "school," a "parking lot," "Navy pier and offices," the fact that my mother was employed there, the meaning of "baseball" and "baseball field," the meaning of a "parking lot," and the meaning behind "being named a top administrator of this new school."

Now as primarily an "intuitive" by nature, my inclination is to jump right from a quick grasp of these symbolic meanings to interpreting the dream. Following the methodology I outlined in the Prologue, that would be a mistake. Best to slow down and look at each concrete dream symbol in as much detail as possible (sensation) in an objective way (what does each symbol mean?) and then go on to figure out the archetypal fields present there and deduce from the fields the archetypes at play and the dominant ones. Finally, one would move into interpretation (translation) and, perhaps, bring in some subjectivity.

Without being too revelatory, I am particularly attracted to the idea of a school and that I would be a top administrator (not necessarily literally). And a school on top of a parking lot that used to be a baseball field of the "padres." Of course, I see myself as a "padre;" that's where I'm "parked." The waters of the unconscious are close by and at least on one level I'd take "mother" here as more the archetypal mother, source of nourishment. I certainly do feel nourished when I'm involved in really significant learning and teaching. So at least initially I'm inclined to think (not that this exhausts the dream meaning), that, as in a former dream considered herein, I need to pursue learning but learning and education that nourishes me and helps me nourish others as well. Since I've also been preoccupied of late with discerning which specific area I am more called to specialize in as a learning and teaching discipline, and since "baseball" is one very specific sport among many, perhaps the dream is also trying to move me to a decision on that.

In terms of "bliss," I do love being engaged in learning and teaching situations. The most nourishing educational ventures for me as a teacher occur when there is meaningful and feeling-toned dialogical exchanges going on between myself and the other participants. This happens most frequently when I am conducting classes with Catholic laypeople interested in getting better prepared for ministry.

My main intent is, nonetheless, not to analyze my dreams but to give you, the reader, some hints together with some practical examples, about how to proceed in working with your own dreams.

I read recently that there's some good indication that dreams appear physiologically as holograms in the brain, and that would indicate the desirability of "circumambulating" the dream so as to take in all the different facets of it, much like one would walk around an artificial hologram. This also indicates the possibility or probability that if the dreamer can capture at least one significant image of a dream, that the rest of the dream is present there too, just as any portion of a holographic image contains the entire image. (See Fred Alan Wolff's The Dreaming Universe, 1994).

In my own experience with dream work and in particular with doing dream work in groups, the temptation many of us fall into is giving into the urgency of looking for the *interpretation*. It seems to me that when people put their vulnerability on the line and share some dream that they mostly need to be "held" and affirmed so that they themselves can relax into their dream and get some insights about it. Also, rather than letting a group churn up subjective interpretations of symbols and metaphors from dreams, it is more productive to proceed on the conviction that the dream means what it says: that there is objectivity there and that this objectivity is what we need to circumambulate around until revelation happens. In other words, it's not about us, the members of the dream group, and it's not even about the dreamer: it's about the dream and about what the dream wants to say.

In this sense, Michael Conforti uses the word "*translation*" more than interpretation, because the idea is to translate the dream's intended meaning from dream symbolism into articulate speech which people can understand. And he continually stresses the objective nature of dreams and the desirability of moving groups away from subjectivity toward an awareness of the psyche's intent to convey something specific and objective, either for the dreamer, or, sometimes, for a larger group, culture or even the world community.

The Spiritual Dimension

Looking at the educators mentioned in this chapter, I think they all offer good theories for learning and living. But from an Augustinian Spirituality perspective they lack something rather essential to life, which is that ultimately we can't by our own power somehow accomplish the goals they set (like being in complete accord with one's Self, or being totally integrated, or knowing absolutely the myth a person needs to live by). Whether a person is seeking liberation from tyranny for some oppressed group or the freeing up of a person with mental or emotional difficulties, or concerned about assisting someone to attain meaning in life: all worthwhile goals, obviously, how can one do this without God's illuminating grace? I would think that without this kind of a reference and without some kind of a living faith that people striving for such lofty goals would eventually lose their zeal and energy unless buttressed by the felt realization that grace is with them. Put another way, even though a practitioner of Rogerian person-centered therapy, or a psychologist working in Logotherapy (Frankl), or an educator using Freire's methodology might not want to admit it, having a prayerful sense of the sacred and a conviction about being graced by God, have a deepening effect on people. We all certainly run the risk of burnout or an exhausted ego, but I believe there's les severity of that for people of faith, at least sufficient faith to be willing to admit one's own powerlessness in the face of addictions and certain impossible situations.

6

ORGANIZATIONAL DEVELOPMENT

Just as I've demonstrated the centrality of interaction/relationship and archetypal activity in the previous chapters, I do so now with respect to organizational development. My main sources here are Margaret Wheatley who continues to provide marvelous leadership in this field, and John Corlett and Carol Pearson. I describe the experience of chaos and how what feels so negative is actually an experience filled with new possibility. I describe the configuration of archetypes in an organizational setting and, finally I offer some thoughts on relational leadership and on the importance of free-flowing information in any enterprise.

Organizational Leadership

An excellent book on this subject is Leadership and the New Science, by Margaret Wheatley. She applies the findings of Quantum Physics and other modern sciences to organizations and, among other things, as in the above areas, concludes the critical importance of being in relationship for the health of one's organization. One of her "specifications" from science is "chaos" and "chaos theory." Probably most of us are familiar with chaos in various ways, both individually and in the groups and organizations to which we belong. Margaret Wheatley makes a good case for looking into chaos for hints, (strange attractors of meaning), about the nature of the order that is trying to emerge.

I find her book both interesting and inspiring. I also appreciate very much what she writes about the application of "Field Theory" to organizational life. Basically she says that those who work in any organization have the power to create either a positive or negative field and that if an organization's work is in the public sector, its clientele can easily pick that up for good or ill. Since I'm in church work, that makes me wonder about the "fields" we create in our environments or that get created unconsciously when we don't pay conscious attention to such phenomena. This also brings up an interesting subject to which O'Murchu alludes in his book Quantum Theology, which is that we participate in creating reality to some extent through our interactions.

Which is not to say that there's no objectivity "out there." People in their various interactions with each other and with the environment in general, do come to some consensus about things: about what is, what should be and what could and ought to be.

And this differs from culture to culture. This, for many cultures today, points to the need for a very broadly based consensus as representing the common expectations of the people. And archetypes are objectively "there" even though experienced subjectively.

So Quantum Theology is not a "solipsism" which denies all objectivity. It does, however, ask us to be aware of the fact that we do help create our social systems, and that we're all called to take part in the dance of life and not just look on as though we are merely observers (Sage archetype). This approach, like Quantum Physics, doesn't absolutize scientific objectivity. The "observer" is always having some effect on the observed.

Margaret Wheatley first published her book Leadership and the New Science in 1992. She revised it and in a preface to the 1999 edition, she writes:

"I believe the fundamental work of this time – work that requires the participation of all of us – is to discover new ways of being together. Our old ways of relating to each other don't sustain us any longer, whether it's at home, in community, at work, or as nation states. I hope that in reading this new edition, you will feel better supported in the work you are already doing, and feel invited to accept new challenges. It is up to us to journey forth in search of new practices and new ideas that will enable us to create lives and organizations worthy of human habitation." (p. xi)

Chaos

Wheatley wonders why organizations aren't working well. My understanding of what she describes in her book leads me to think that the reason organizations aren't working well is that we don't understand the underlying dynamics of organizational life. That is, old models of organizations taken from Newtonian physics, which is mechanistic and materialistic, just don't fit. The new sciences are telling us that all life is holistic and integrative, and that apparent chaos in organizations is best looked at as a necessary reordering rather than a sign of demise.

Organized religion in developed countries is today in a state of chaos in terms of leadership, sexual issues in general and celibacy requirements in particular, the equality of men and women, and the tendency of the churches to perpetuate patriarchal values and structures. A Quantum approach to leadership has much to offer the churches and other institutions as well in this regard and would, I believe, help them navigate the chaos.

Chaos Theory posits that in the midst of chaos, the beginnings of a new organizing principle are already present. But one needs to look for it and then cooperate in so far as possible to bring it to birth. The organizing principle is called a "strange attractor." I suggest that one strange attractor at work today in the midst of religious chaos is "community" with all that word implies, including, most basically, relating in a dialogical fashion as a significant trait of all involved in any given religious enterprise.

Relational Leadership

Leadership is being considered in this new paradigm for its relational aspects.

"At the personal level, many authors write now on our interior relationship with our spirit, soul, and life's purpose. Ecological writers stress the relationship that exists not only between us and all beings in our environment, but also between future generations and us. If the physics of our time is revealing the primacy of relationships, is it any wonder that we are beginning to rethink our major issues in more relational terms?" (Wheatley, p. 14)

Some interesting observations on leadership come from psychological typology. For example, an SJ leader would tend to emphasize the importance and centrality of the institution. An SP leader would be concerned that there be constant activity; an NT type would tend to be interested in precision; and the NF would be concerned that the people for whom she or he is leader find their tasks meaningful. Mix in with the above the further complications of Perception and Judging and you get either an emphasis from the leader on planning (J) or on spontaneity (P).

Whatever a person's leadership style, all people are by nature "relational." That is, people grow, maintain emotional and psychological health, and become themselves through relationships, both personal and professional. If a person in a position of leadership would stifle this relational dimension or minimize it, this might indicate some serious pathology or personality disorder. I think at the least it would indicate unsuitability for leadership. At the same time, one does well to bring to conscious awareness the possibility of getting entrained into others' archetypal fields and thus losing sight of one's own values, thoughts and positions.

Information

In her book, Wheatley writes extensively about the "nature" of information. It is, she concludes, the very energy of the organization. So if information flow is controlled or manipulated or somehow not given free and open expression throughout an organization, the consequences may be quite damaging. In her experience, management often tries to keep a tight lid on what information gets out to the rest of the organization. It is her conviction that an organization will thrive and keep on reorganizing itself at more efficient levels when there is free flow of information in all directions. One can appreciate some similarity here with the liberating education ideas of Paulo Freire. (One might be thinking of the sexual abuse crisis affecting the churches. Free flow of information would do much to alleviate the situation).

Margaret Wheatley, in her research, tries to discover what makes organizations work. What she discovers is that relationship is the most fundamental aspect of organizational life and therefore that which requires most attention. So if information flow is restricted or in some way distorted, the underlying issue will most likely have to do with the quality of relationships in the organization's membership. And whenever we have questions of relationship, somewhere there are archetypes, and in reality it is the archetypes and their respective fields that most demand our attention.

Mapping the Organizational Psyche

Corlett and Pearson, in their book by the same name as this section, offer twelve archetypes they consider active in organizations and they divide them into four categories. These categories and their archetypes are: People (Everyperson, Jester & Lover); Learning (Innocent, Sage & Explorer); Results (Magician, Revolutionary & Hero); and Stabilizing (Creator, Caregiver & Ruler). People and Results are in tension with each other as are Stabilizing and Learning. The tension comes from a certain oppositional focus. For example, an organization must have stabilizing rules and procedures and other elements that help an office and its personnel function smoothly and efficiently. New learning coming into the organization may well disturb office equilibrium. Likewise, an organization aims at producing some "product" whether concretely or more symbolically as in a service industry. Does one put more importance on the product or on the people involved, both personnel and the public served? People, Learning, Results and Stabilizing are referred to by the authors of the Mapping book, as "faces."

Organizational Unconscious

In 2004 I started to learn about and experience the Assisi Conferences and Seminars (now called the Assisi Institute). Their main center is in Brattleboro, Vermont. They offer continuing education for psychotherapists (esp. of the Jungian persuasion), organizational consultants, and other interested professionals. Of special interest to me is their approach to organizational consultation that stresses looking for patterns and for the underlying archetypes that are getting constellated in the organization. Using other terms, one would be looking for the unconscious of the organization and how certain unconscious archetypal influences are impacting it. The Assisi Conferences also bring in the findings of the new sciences and show how quantum thought and other theories can also be helpful in organizational consultation. As I previously wrote in this paper, the founder and principal spokesperson of the Assisi Institute is Dr. Michael Conforti.

One central objective at the Assisi Institute is to convey the teaching that organizations are like individuals: they also have an unconscious and all the archetypes that an individual has (or which have an individual). They have Ego, Persona, Shadow and Self, and are either more Anima or Animus, and they show through their Ego other developmental archetypes, out of four different "faces": learning, results, people and stability.

Archetypal Field Pattern Reading

If one can determine after some lengthy and in-depth observation and analysis of some situation that one is faced with a pattern, chances are good that one is dealing with a field behind which is an archetype. This can be a pattern in a dream, or a pattern evident in someone's life, or a pattern in some group or organizational setting. One does best to sit with the pattern for as long as possible to let it sink in before attempting to interpret it or seek to translate it. And one is taking in the pattern not only intellectually but also making use of feeling and intuition so that the reality of the pattern is grasped as completely as possible. This pattern reading is what the organizational ego does in looking to surface the unconscious of itself.

The ultimate question for both individuals and organizations to confront, is: what is wanted for me or for us? This has to do with Self. We know objectively what is wanted: that we get the conscious part of us to relate as much as possible with our unconscious, with Shadow, Anima/Animus, other archetypal energies and with the Self. But the Self also has *particular* desires and plans. Figuring that out is of great importance and has to do with one's individuation, either as an individual or an organization. And sometimes the archetypal fields that are impacting a person or organization will provide helpful hints about the movements and desires of the Self.

Though this kind of psychological language comes out of Jung's mapping of the soul, Augustine would have no problem navigating in these waters. He would not, however, as Jung does (and maybe must, as a psychologist), put the stress on consciousness; he would put it on a more fundamental reality: God's grace working in human persons and communities and institutions and our need to cooperate with the movements of grace and not insist that somehow or other *we* are in charge. And Augustine would insist too that we must live *with* and *in* a certain amount of uncertainty and not claim for our understanding what is beyond us, veiled in mystery, like God's nature as Trinity, or the Incarnation of Logos as Jesus of Nazareth. The dilemma is that we still must speak of these things and speculate on how best to describe and understand them, yet without claiming understanding, for we are seeing as though looking into a cloudy mirror (to paraphrase St. Paul). (These observations are largely from Fr. Robert Dodaro during his classes on Augustinian Spirituality, Feb., 2012).

7

NEW SYNTHESIS, NEW MYTH

In this chapter I am principally concerned with presenting some of the key ideas of Diarmuid O'Murchu since he himself has come up with a way of describing a new myth for our times based on the new sciences and with consistent theological nuances and implications. I especially allude to the twelve principles found in his book Quantum Theology. To help with some understanding of "myth" I also bring in some contributions of Joseph Campbell and Carl Jung in this regard, as well as of the psychiatrist Victor Frankl. Finally I pose some of the difficulties connected with historicity and myth.

Now since all is from the divine in some way or other, whether in matter or organizational development, education, psychology or sociology or some form of counseling, I think all can be subsumed under the umbrella of theology. As I see it, this is the still embryonic phenomenon called "Quantum Theology," that place where the lines demarcating intellectual disciplines and fields of thought become quite blurred. I also feel inclined to use the term "Quantum Psychology" and having in mind just about the same content. In fact, since "theologies" tend to be sectarian and imply to some extent, acts of faith and doctrinal adherence, maybe "Quantum Psychology" is a more exact term. At least to my way of thinking, "what is needed" is not a new or different set of "beliefs," but rather a new if emerging reasonable and empirical paradigm around which people can unite, whatever their religious beliefs.

Quantum Theology, the Book

Diarmuid O'Murchu, a priest and social psychologist living in London, wrote a book by the same name (Quantum Theology) in 1997. Here are some excerpts from his book:

"Fuzziness, uncertainty, and probability are the crucial features of existence at this deeper, quantum level where...we are dealing with a piece of action best described as a set of relationships." (p.29) "The Reign of God...is the central myth of the New Testament...It is an invitation to work for a new world order, marked by right relationships of justice, love, peace and liberation." (Pp. 115, 116)

A good way to get at the fundamentals of this book is to discuss the "Principles of Quantum Theology." I think if you engage these principles, and better still, if you read and absorb the book itself, you'll see how all-encompassing the subject is, how ecumenical and inter-faith, and embracing of the other disciplines I've mentioned. You'll also see the centrality of relationship in all areas of existence. O'Murchu lists twelve principles and specifies each principle in what he calls "new elements." If you want to gain some understanding of these principles, discuss them with some others. Again, the best approach is to use the book Quantum Theology as a tool and study these principles in context.

O'Murchu ends his book with the following paragraph:

"When we let go of our patriarchal props, categories, labels, powers, and "certainties," we don't abandon ourselves to the "forces of evil." Perhaps for the first time we encounter the relational God at the heart of a relational universe, albeit one that today is emaciated with the pain of so much wrecked relatedness. We too are relational creatures. We belong to a greater whole, held forever in the gracious embrace of divine abandonment. In letting go of our patriarchal securities, we come home to where we really belong, to the universe itself. Here, love, and not fear, is the enduring reality!" (Pp. 206, 207)

Campbell

An American author, teacher and "Mythologist" (now deceased) who advised George Lucas on the content of the Star Wars series, Joseph Campbell by name, should also be mentioned here. Like the other thinkers already alluded to, Campbell too is interested in that which is common to all cultures and peoples. His specific area of interest is in how we are all moved from within by our innate archetypes: for example, by that archetype which has to do with the hero and heroine.

I think a good model for the hero/heroine archetype is the quaternity I mentioned above in Chapter 3, Depth Psychology. That is, people are called to develop their hero/heroine aspects in congruence with their personality and character type. So a person may be a hero or heroine as parent, or studious type, or warrior or lover. Or one may use the twelve archetypes offered by Carol Pearson that are specific instances or incarnations of the hero-heroine general archetype. The first challenge for people is to discover their basic personality and character type. The second is to have the courage to resist the culture and other people who may want to force them into a different way of being, as, for example, a father who wants a warrior son or a culture and school system which only reward extraverted behavior.

Like Carl Jung, Campbell places much importance on the religious instinct, the presence of the inner God-image (Self) and the search for meaning by following one's own bliss, whatever that might be (and "bliss" is not to be confused with always following the desires of Ego). When people are not consciously in touch with the myths in and out of which they live, their lives lose meaning and purpose. Individuals, groups and entire cultures can lose their myths. It is my conviction that the Holon in particular and Quantum Theology in general, are providing us with a new collective myth. It is, of course, still the responsibility of individuals to discover and embrace their particularization of this more general myth.

Carl Jung was also greatly interested in the importance of "myth." In fact, he thought that the Europe of his time (and, I presume, he would have the same opinion about contemporary European culture), had lost its myth and so had lost its meaning. More concretely, he was of the view that Christianity was no longer a living, vital force for the majority of European people. Yet he was also convinced that people have a religious instinct and that they need a Myth as a framework for living that out.

I'm not sure if Jung took that another step, but it seems to me he did in his reflections on alcoholism: that the religious instinct will manifest in some other, sometimes bizarre or perverse ways, if it is not able to be expressed in a religious form. I would imagine that would explain at least in part other addictions as well, e.g., sexual addictions, food addiction, addictions to drugs, etc. Perhaps even codependency stems from some frustration of the religious instinct.

From his experience as a psychotherapist, Jung recommended to his patients that they consider returning to the religion of their childhood (he didn't mean that literally; rather a return to the spiritual values of one's religious tradition); he was convinced that ultimately no cure would last without the embracing of a religious myth in some form.

I would concretize Jung's critique of organized religion further by suggesting that to the extent any religion stifles the free flow of information (see Chapter on Communication), and insists on a culture of silence and secrecy, that such behaviors and the attitudes underlying them are pathological and are sowing the seeds of self-destruction in that religion.

Frankl

The psychologist Victor Frankl (one of our professors in the School of Human Behavior at U.S.I.U. in San Diego, now Alliant International Univ.) engages the same theme in his well-known book Man's Search for Meaning, though with some differences. I don't think Frankl would subscribe to the idea of returning to the religion of one's childhood as the answer to lack of meaning. For Frankl, people must, in effect, create or discover their own personal myth and make a firm decision about embracing it. In other words, for him people decide what their myth is and the myth then becomes a source of meaning. Appropriately enough, his system is called "Logotherapy" or "healing through meaning." I believe a person suffering from lack of meaning might find Frankl's ideas most helpful.

Historicity and Myth

I have come to appreciate the work of the Jesus Seminar scholars in their efforts to investigate the historicity of the Gospels. Of course it has been a challenge for me to have to come to grips with their conclusions about what is historical and what is not, especially regarding texts I always presumed to be historically verifiable. But interestingly enough, getting some clarity in the area of historicity of texts has greatly increased my appreciation for the "mythic" element. What I mean by that is, that in some cases it doesn't really matter whether or to what extent a passage is historical: it can still be true in other ways (theologically, mythically and/or metaphorically) and so have an effect on the hearer or reader. I do have some concern about people delving into Jesus Seminar studies without adequate, critical preparation and skills because they might find it too much for them to deal with and perhaps find their faith weakened

When we say something is true "mythically" we mean that hearing the story or reading it, one's archetypes come alive, you identify readily with some or even all of the characters of a text (e.g., the Prodigal Son), you feel spiritually enlivened, and the Word has become a source of meaning in a soulful sort of way.

I also appreciate delving into the historicity of the gospels because of the difficulty I've had with trying to understand how Jesus could have said or done (as in the "nature" miracles), certain things. Realizing that many controversial texts came, in fact, from other sources makes it easier to deal with them. Otherwise I find myself going through mental gymnastics trying to square texts with the person of the historical Jesus, as I understand him. Perhaps the sacred texts of other religions are also better understood when read critically and with a view toward distinguishing the factually historical from the metaphoric.

Again, here we are dealing with "relativity." That is, the scriptural authors write with certain presuppositions or prejudices about the nature of things and these presuppositions inevitably color much of their material. This aspect of the text is, then, "relative" to the period in which it was written. Then the hearers and readers of the texts come along and they bring their points of view along with them. So how does one find a way out of the relativity dilemma? Through engaging with others around the content and meaning of the texts, making use of experts in the original languages of the writings, on linguistics, biblical archeology and other sciences which seek deeper understandings of the texts.

I think too that belonging to the community of the Church and having a commitment to the receiving and passing on of the Tradition is a kind of saving grace when one gets a bit confused due to difficulties in scriptural understanding and interpretation. For first and foremost, the scripture, in particular the New Testament, is the Church's book: the

Church existed prior to the writings and decided which of many texts would comprise its sacred book.

Quantum

To get at the essence of a quantum approach is to picture whatever reality one is looking at as a hologram. Then one attempts to examine this hologram from as many different aspects as possible. What this approach does is help a person get as holistic a picture as possible of something thereby assisting one with avoiding getting too focused on just one area which, in turn, will prove useful in coming to grips with one's complexes. This is so because a complex arises due to a narrow view of some reality often due to the ego's urge to be the center of attention (thus a "persona" or some other complex). In a general sense we are dealing here with the desirability of increased consciousness and suggesting that a tool for achieving this is through the imaginal construction of holograms and thus relativizing ego control and urges. This can also be viewed as an exercise in obsession, but a conscious one, and a kind of obsessing around some object of interest which one has habitually looked at only partially. With more of the whole truth about some obsession, the obsessing can be diffused and the complex weakened and the archetype behind the complex healthfully integrated into consciousness.

Dream Themes

Sometimes you might find a particular theme running through your dreams. My own dreams often picture me, sometimes alone, sometimes with others, in large churches celebrating Christian Eucharist. At times in these dreams I have difficulty remembering where I'm at in the service or sometimes the people get up and leave, or I forget what I'm going to say in a homily. Sometimes the churches are old and decrepit and sometimes they are new and full of life. (Do you have on-going themes in your dreams)?

What I consider most important about the above is that the dreams I mention demonstrate a certain pattern, and that from such a pattern that one can infer an archetypal field and thus some underlying archetype or archetypes. And, to become conscious of the primary patterns, fields and archetypes acting in one's life, to see their meanings and learn from them about one's own calling, destiny and fate, represents a big step on the road to individuation.

I do think there is a Quantum/Newtonian factor influencing many people in the ways they view their religion and religious practice. One example of this is the great emphasis some Catholics put on The Catechism of the Catholic Church. Here we have a definitive and relatively up to date compendium of Catholic teaching clearly and unambiguously stated. I'm sure many people find this book to be a very popular and handy source for their religious guidance. This is a good example of the Newtonian, explicate world in a religious context. The other side of this in the Catholic tradition is what has historically been referred to as "speculative theology." Those more interested in this side of things will probably not have much interest in the Catechism. Yet, from a purely objective point of view, I think both are important, and sometimes one and the same person might well see the value of both sides, the value of a definitive text of belief, and the value of an on-going conversation on Christian teaching and spirituality which seeks to further unpack the implicate order relative to Christianity.

Having had for several years engaged in parish ministry and adult religious education, my impression is that the great majority of active parishioners are mainly interested in feeling contained and supported in their religious and spiritual lives. In the present context this means that most parishioners are Newtonian primarily (or think they are) and that they do not have much interest getting into the depths of things either religiously or philosophically. So adult education programs of a more speculative nature will attract and hold a very small percentage of a parish population. Most parishioners are content with Sunday Mass and a short homily and really are not usually interested in being challenged in their beliefs or in even learning how to articulate them in a more adult fashion.

An Old Myth

Using the language of the New Sciences, one is constructing what appears to be a new myth. There are antecedents to this, however, especially in Hinduism. But part of the new myth or paradigm is old, dating from the Hebrew and Christian scriptures with their emphasis on being of service to and living with concern for the least among us, and especially from the Acts of the Apostles with its emphasis on community. This all has to do with the "spirituality" part of the new paradigm, the Augustinian part which has many components and which sees the grace of God as also intrinsic to the project. See Chapters 12 and 13 especially for more on this subject.

8

COMMUNICATION

There are some significant obstacles to good communication that therefore greatly limit our human attempts at relationship. One of these is the "borderline" disorder. Another source sometimes of such obstacles is the very environment in which we live. Yet another is the basic worldview which people use as "lenses" through which they view "reality." I write briefly of "Daoism" here as an antidote to our dualistic tendencies and I also offer some insights from 12-step programs (especially Co-dependents Anonymous) as very helpful in improving communication.

I want to say something about "interaction" from a kind of philosophical point of view. Sometimes what appears to be interaction can be an attempt, conscious or unconscious, to obfuscate. And some people can communicate quite well without a great deal of verbal interaction. And there are some people with whom any communication around important issues can be quite dangerous. This might be the case, for instance, when you're with people whose world view is totally at variance with your own and who want to impose their thinking on you, if possible, by ranting and raving or some more subtle form of arm-twisting. You know who they are and you guard your interactions accordingly. I don't mean to imply that there are people whom all others must avoid contact with; rather, the point is, that for each person there are some others who are "dangerous" to one for any number of factors. That of course is a most unpleasant experience but I think rather common.

On the other hand, if you've ever had the occasion to be in communication with someone who is describing an overwhelming experience of having felt surrounded and filled with God's presence, a kind of "peak experience," or however one may prefer to describe this kind of phenomenon, then you know how enchanting communication can be at times. I consider this one example of communication (interaction) wherein the presence of the archetypal (Self, in this case), is quite palpable and energizing. I would extend this notion to include any and all communication that can make explicit the archetype or archetypes that are present. In counseling sessions, spiritual direction and education in spirituality, it is precisely those moments of archetypal movement which create the most favorable climate for learning and growth. Spiritual directors, counselors and teachers of spirituality would do very well indeed to concentrate on the uncovering of archetypes in their ministries for that reason. This is the most natural and most human, most physical basis for movements of the Spirit in one's life, and also for the life of groups and organizations. I want to reiterate that looking into archetypal fields is, in effect, getting "behind the scenes," and seeing reality in its most profound depth. No doubt there are people who are quite content just looking at appearances and dealing with that. But for those people not satisfied with just manifest reality, looking into the world of archetypes may be the way to go.

Borderline Disorders

What I have to say here is related to the paragraph above in Chapter 3 on Narcissism. Again, this is not meant to unduly criticize or judge those with these disorders; in fact, we all to some extent or other share in them. Rather, the more one can recognize these traits in oneself and others, the more one can take them into account, maybe work on them and at least be aware of their dynamics when in interactions of various kinds with oneself and others. The term "borderline" refers to a lack of clear boundaries. This may take the form of either being too permeable to other people's influence or of being too closed off to others. Put another way, one may be too easily influenced and naïve or too distanced and unreachable. In either case there is a fundamental problem in relating and this problem can often be traced to early narcissistic wounding.

This is a very difficult issue to deal with both by the person with the disorder, with family and friends and with counselors and psychotherapists. Some psychotherapists specialize in this disorder and I think it's best to refer to them when up against this kind of distress. I mention this here because like narcissism, a borderline-afflicted person tends to distort communication. Every comment and gesture is self-referenced; objectivity is very difficult to come by; trust is almost non-existent. This is not true in every case, but frequently there has been a history of incest or other serious abuse in the lives of these people. Great care is needed in ordinary conversation with them and great compassion too.

When communication is called for and really needs to happen, refusal to engage another can have disastrous results. Countless people have felt driven crazy, some even to psychosis, by having to be with people who would not communicate. Perhaps we all know people who avoid necessary communication, or even families and other groups living in such darkness.

Environment

Whatever one's psychological type is would have some bearing on their communication style, especially the extravert/introvert factor. But in terms of *what* is communicated, I imagine home life and early education are more crucial, especially parental modeling. There are also cultural factors in that people do hand on from generation to generation certain central values surrounding communication, as, for example, in the maxim, "If you don't have anything to say, don't say anything at all;" and, "don't hang your dirty laundry out in public." So some people learn very early on not to talk about certain subjects, or even almost not to speak at all except on relatively innocuous subjects.

Two World Views

In Western thought until the thirteenth century, more or less, most European people simply accepted the prevailing world-view called Platonic: that there's more out there than meets the eye or can be discerned by the senses; that there's some sort of spiritual reality of which this world we see is a dim reflection. By contrast there is the Aristotelian view that is basically materialistic: "what you see is what you get and that's all there is." The Platonic view was espoused by St. Augustine and the Aristotelian view was largely lost until rediscovered in Bagdad and then Islamic Spain by Jewish, Islamic and Christian scholars and introduced into Christian Europe by way of Thomas Aquinas (who absorbed it from Albert the Great, his teacher), at the University of Paris. Eventually this view gained precedence that resulted in a dualistic view of Christianity and spirituality and eventually in the Deism, materialism and secularism of the Age of Reason (c.1700 on). Of course, this is summary and overly simplistic, and Aristotelians should not be dismissed as somehow lacking depth.

Yet, the question is: can you communicate with someone who holds tenaciously to an Aristotelian notion of reality when you hold the opposite? How deeply can you communicate with another whose world-view is so different you don't even hold to the same beliefs about the nature of reality? The notion of "archetypes" and their objectivity comes to us from Plato, ultimately, and that reality consists of much more than simply meets the senses.

Daoism http://simple.wikipedia.org/wiki/Taoism

Cultures in other parts of the world have not suffered from a dualistic tendency nearly as much as those of the West. There's a philosophical/religious system from China called Daoism. In that system everything is seen as process and movement. The symbol of the Dao expresses it graphically: in what are apparently opposites there is always something of the other present in each; a bit of light in the darkness, a bit of dark in the light; a bit of the feminine in the masculine, etc. So our categories of "opposites" are illusory if they are seen too concretely as representing the way things really are.

Daoism fits well with the Quantum view that all is connected, that the observer affects the observed, and that what is "out there" is also "in here."

12-Step Programs

If sometimes in seeking to communicate with another you feel your personal integrity being threatened, try a technique offered by the 12-step movement: say to yourself and be convinced: "I am not responsible for the way *you* think or feel nor am I responsible for what you may think of me or anyone else." That's certainly a boundary setter and can come in handy when someone singles you out for verbal abuse or in some way exhibits rage. You don't have to take responsibility for another's addictions, including their addiction to rage. It may or may not be a good idea to communicate these sentiments to the other, but at least this kind of conviction can help one establish some suitable boundaries when communicating with difficult people.

Rage, like alcohol and other drugs, can be addictive. And addictions inhibit communication and so go against living according to a quantum paradigm. In 12-step meetings, whether a speaker's meeting or book study or group sharing, the participants gradually come to accept their addictions and figure out what to do about them.

Codependency

One type of 12-step program (and they are many and various) is aimed at helping people with codependency issues. That term refers to a tendency to confuse and intermingle oneself too much with some other or others to the extent of losing one's own identity. This is the person who is overly helpful and solicitous for others to his or her own detriment. They let other people walk all over them and need to be needed. Here's an example of how the codependent person thinks: "I don't care how *I* feel; I care how *you* feel."

Having to relate with a person with this addiction to others is experienced as draining. You might feel like you're being stalked or harassed and, unless the codependency is mutual, you will probably avoid this person.

A Dream

Prompted by some complaints and observations made by Bill X, the members of the Western province of Augustinians are asked to fill out a questionnaire relative to our work. It seems that mainly it has to do with St. Augustine High School. In working on my responses I notice we are near the sea and some of the time I am wading in a tide pool.

Then I'm in a classroom at the school wearing the Augustinian habit and snapping the long belt in a joking way as though I'm prepared to whip unruly students. I am surprised to see the class is mixed, boys and girls, since the school's always been just for boys. My impression is that a lady who is there is in charge of the class and that I'm there just to add some flavor and to help the kids with their work. A lad arrives late walking slowly with the aid of a walker. In spite of his handicap the teacher is very strict and tells him he can't be late and to go back home.

I've introduced several dreams in the course of this paper. You may wonder why. For the most part, at least in our North American English-speaking culture, people tend to stay on the surface of things. That's not very nourishing, of course, and hopefully there are times when all people get more deep with themselves and others about their concerns and their lives in general. But with dreams one cannot avoid the depths. I'm not too prepared to get much into this dream, but I wonder about the "tide pool" and my own tendency to stay in the shallows and so avoid the depths. From 1966 to 1972, when I taught in high schools, there was a presumption that discipline was to be maintained with force. I never much liked that idea and, "gracias a Dios," times change. The boy in the dream is somehow handicapped. Part of dream theory sees all the characters in a dream as somehow having to do with the dreamer, so I'd have to ask myself how I am handicapped, or unable to get to "class." And why is the lady teacher in the dream being so strict and seemingly unfeeling? And what is meant here symbolically? Whatever the answers to these questions, I have the feeling I'm again confronted with the notion of the desirability for me of educational experiences whether as instructor or student that are nurturing. How does this dream of mine speak to you?

I want to stress again, in this section, that some people live more out of a Newtonian framework and consciousness, and others more out of a Quantum consciousness. To put this another way, for some people that is really real which is observable and measurable (explicate), and for others that which is really real is hidden (implicate) and unobservable. I think we tend to be with and relate mostly with those who share our own preferences in this regard. And some people tend to even demonize those on the other side. Thus the epithets "bean counter" and "space cadet." What is often lost sight of is that we all simply have to live in both worlds whatever our natural inclinations.

Applying this to organizations, it seems to me that in order to move toward ever greater organizational wholeness, any given enterprise would want to do both a quantitative (Newtonian) and a qualitative (Quantum) depth self analysis. The quantitative assessment would look at all the organization's measurable components, and the qualitative one would tease out such immeasurables as psychological typology, the faces of the organization and its primary developmental archetypes, the balance of masculine and feminine energies, the Self of the organization, its persona, the composition of its organizational ego, and other intangibles. Very likely the leadership behind such an assessment would be composed of more Newtonian-oriented people for the quantitative study and of more Quantum-oriented people for the qualitative part.

Individuals from time to time have the experience of losing touch with their Selves. The quest to reestablish that connection can be very stressful, and in my opinion, can't happen by human will alone but comes about rather by grace, by the Transcendent Function, which is to say, by God's initiative. This is an experience not easily forgotten.

And organizations have similar experiences. They too once in a while lose touch with their primary purpose, which is to say, with the organizational Self. Thus the value of a depth approach to help organizations reconnect. Again, no easy task. I don't suppose many traditional consultants suggest this, but it seems to me a very good idea for those who make up the organizational ego of some such organization, to spend some time praying for their organization, and in particular in asking the Source of all things to help them reconnect to the organizational Self.

This may not make much sense to people operating primarily out of a mechanistic Newtonian framework, but it will feel right and very congruent to those who are at home in the Quantum world where intentions mean a lot and where people have the ability to construct fields and patterns intentionally and the power to activate desired archetypes in the collective unconscious of their organization. It just makes good sense: if you love your organization, you'll pray for it.

9

THEOLOGIES

In this chapter, I argue for the on-going creation of an ecumenical theology as a way to provide a basis for dialogue among people of different faiths, and I present some obstacles to the use of such a theology. I suggest that I have offered in this paper an outline for this. I also show how an ethical system can be developed out of this quantum approach, which can offer some insights into, for example, sexual ethics, the ethical implications of dogmatism, and the crucial importance of friendship in leading an ethical life. Finally, I describe some reflections on St. Augustine who, after Jesus and St. Paul, has had more influence on Western thought over the centuries than any other historical figure. My observations on Augustine and on iconography in this and other chapters largely come from a three-month diploma course on Augustinian Spirituality offered at Colegio Santa Monica in Rome by the Order of St. Augustine in 2012 (Feb., March & April).

An Ecumenical Theology

It's in the nature of my work that I usually interact professionally mostly with Catholic people. I find among more educated Catholics a strong conviction that, at their best, theologies draw people together rather than apart. Quantum Theology is not the same as a Catholic Theology. Yet it is not in opposition to it. I see it rather as providing a reality-based cosmology and philosophy for all theologies open to an ecumenical and inter-religious perspective. It's rather like science and religion: at their best these two areas are not in opposition, but complement each other.

Quantum Theology (or, if you prefer Quantum Psychology), is a way of perceiving reality, which can provide a basis for ecumenical and inter-religious exchange while still respecting specific theological positions which may be at variance with one's own religion. Quantum Theology seeks to provide a metaphor and a language whereby people can speak with each other in a search for common ground. If you look into the Quantum approach and find there's some area that doesn't fit your understanding of your own specific denominational theology that might well be a fruitful area for you to look into. You might find that your understanding is out of line, or you might conclude that there's something in Quantum Theology that just doesn't seem congruent with your belief system, or it's possible you won't be able to get a good "fit" in that particular area.

I understand Quantum Theology to be an "umbrella" under which many "theologies" can fit comfortably: e.g., feminism, theologies of liberation, creation-centered theology and eco-theology. And, since the primary revelation of the divine is in and through nature, all the other facets and disciplines of human life and understanding are also accommodated within this paradigm.

In the Quantum approach, cooperation and collaboration are much to be preferred to competition, and the values of domination traditionally ascribed to a patriarchal consciousness are heartily rejected.

People of any religion who feel a need to see their particular religious system as "the only true faith" and who conceive of the divine as somehow restricted to their formulations, won't be very pleased with a quantum theological perspective. It might be helpful to such people to ask themselves about the foundations of their fundamentalism and literalism: is it possibly based on an exaggerated need for certitude? Does it come out of a childish need to see one's own group as the best and most favored? Or does this narrowness come out of a fear that everything is falling apart, that the only path to personal and institutional survival is dogmatism and intolerance?

While presuming that both clergy and laity with such closed and protectionist world-views are well intentioned, it is my conviction that their expressed concerns about religious indifferentism are ill founded. One can be committed to one's own faith and even wish other people would come to share it, while looking for common ground with people of other faiths and appreciating the underlying archetypes present in all the great religious traditions.

Of course if people are unsure in their own religious convictions, they will feel insecure and uncomfortable in inter-religious or ecumenical activities.

Deism

Another possibility is that of "deism." This means that a person conceives of the divine as though a specific entity off beyond the clouds somewhere in anthropomorphic form with "his" definite favorites and immutable will. From a Judeo-Christian point of view, this is idolatry. Nevertheless I think many people of these traditions do conceive of God in this fashion. And whereas those with a more open, ecumenical perspective and commitment to the brotherhood/sisterhood of all people find joy and challenge in inter-religious dialogue, "deists" may well find that they don't have much to dialogue about unless they can begin to conceptualize the divine in other less anthropomorphic ways.

As with descriptions of other pathologies in this paper, here too we must not become too judgmental since this would preclude any possibility of meaningful engagement with these persons. Also, we might find ourselves one day, due to our own fears and insecurities, moving in the same direction, and I'm sure we would not want to simply be dismissed out of hand.

A Theory of Everything

The more I ponder and try to understand Quantum Theology and something of the science which underlies it, the more it seems to me to be more an approach, or itself a sort of paradigm more than content. It provides a way of perceiving and of thinking about the divine, religions, society and culture and the inner workings of the human person. It is quite a challenge to try to keep everything available to consciousness at once. Thus, one would avoid thinking in dualistic terms and would rather consider all things as somehow united, aware of one's own and the other's psychological make-up and culture. One would seek to comprehend something of the New Sciences and the metaphor of the Holon as a New Paradigm, and to keep the centrality of "relationship" and accompanying archetypes always in mind. To keep all this available to one's consciousness is no small task. It even sounds impossible. But to try to line oneself up to do it, to consider this a major life goal and work toward it, given one's capacities, is possible and, I think desirable. And I think one can say that Quantum Theology gets at and describes the way things really are in the "field" that stands behind particular belief systems.

Ethics

If one would take the main metaphors used in this paper as a basis for ethical decision-making, one would come up with something like the following: morality has to do with our relationships with all things: ourselves, other people, the divine, animals and plant species, the earth itself and all the universe (the holon); there is a moral imperative for us to become as conscious of all this as we possibly can, both as individuals and as groups and organizations, because lack of consciousness leads individuals, groups and organizations to project onto others the sorts of things they avoid looking at in themselves (shadow); we are called, again both individually and as groups and organizations, to positively seek the betterment of others, since not to behave with that kind of intentionality runs the risk of negatively influencing the many environments in which we live (fields). Knowing that this is an impossible task for unaided human will and reason, as believers we can, nonetheless, rely on the divine to make up for us what we are lacking. One of the healthiest activities one can engage in is to admit powerlessness in the face of such a daunting task, as one would with an addiction, and then ask for help in facing the challenge.

Morality is not just individual; it is also collective and systemic, which means that we are morally required to work for a more just local, regional, national and international social system in so far as that is within our capacity. A comprehensive moral principle which logically flows from quantum theory is this: seek good, open, honest communication with all others and with yourself and avoid any interaction which would be destructive of such communication and therefore of community. And, be realistic about when such communication is simply not possible. Even on a micro scale, some particles seek relationship and union, while others avoid relating and contact.

Sexuality and Relationship

I think the area of sexual ethics can also be elucidated by the quantum approach. For example, the desire to be sexual with another is often a rather complicated matter. Are the people involved aware of the likelihood of "projections" being present (shadow)? Are they aware that the intensity of this greatly charged situation (Eros) might well affect their other relationships and their work as well (fields)? Are they aware that their state of "possession" is having an impact on the quality of their other interactions (holon)? And yet, is God not present even in such attraction? Anyone interested in pursuing this theme in detail would do well to read Invisible Partners, by the priest psychotherapist John Sanford.

Hate and indifference would certainly qualify as serious sin in the Quantum approach to ethical behavior. To hate or be indifferent poisons the atmosphere (fields), and is destructive of relationships which are of the very essence of the great web of which we are all part. And, of course, to hate the creation is to hate the Maker of it all "in whom we live and move and have our being."

Play and Belief

When you watch children at play, you might perceive a certain seriousness. I propose that spirituality and religion are best experienced within this framework of play and playfulness (Jester). The serious is not excluded, but an intense, scientific, meticulous examining of human conduct and belief with a view toward absolute perfection and the rooting out of all error (Donatism), lack of precision and shadow, doesn't travel well with a spiritual, religious quest. A certain mental, physical and emotional relaxing comes from a playful heart, whether this is in prayer or religious rituals and celebrations or in the articulation of belief and doctrine. Of course this can be taken too far; ritual can be trivialized and spirituality reduced to the infantile. But the Reign of God has been likened to the spirit of the child.

In this context, dogmatism can be viewed as a seriously dangerous path.

Dogmatism is a perception of belief that tends to identify the object of belief with the words used to formulate it as though there's nothing more to be said. This is a kind of idolatry, which seeks exactness and precision where none is to be found and where the better spirit is one of inquiry and openness.

A doctrine is best seen as a pointer, a sort of roadmap indicating a direction, but it ought not be seen as the final word or an end in itself.

Prayer

Whether as an intentional focus of oneself toward the divine or as a felt, spontaneous being-taken-over by what feels spiritual and numinous, many people express an interest as to whether and to what extent, prayer can affect archetypal fields. There is the phenomenon of exorcism in which someone or a group of people claims to drive out the demonic from a person who attests to some diabolical possession. My conviction is that even in these cases what we are dealing with are archetypes and their fields (there *is* archetypal evil often personified in religions as demons). For whatever reason or causes, the person feels unable to handle or integrate an experience, so exorcism or something similar is undertaken.

One outcome of focused, intentional prayer is a heightened consciousness such that often the person praying or others in the prayer field become better able to understand what's going on and name and integrate it.

Sexualities

It seems best to leave questions of sexual morality up to the churches and spiritualities and each person's conscience. I don't believe this is an area of compelling interest to the state. Nor do I think it particularly enhancing spiritually to inquire into another's sexual fantasies, preferences or activity. At the same time people ought to be free to let their friends and companions know of these things, if they so wish, especially where there exists a climate of trust and acceptance. A Quantum Paradigm would encourage open, honest communication and for that people need at least a modicum of stability and societal acceptance.

Friendship

Among all possible relationships and ways of relating, I think that of "friendship" is the most rewarding and long-lasting. Ideally, friendship would precede the commitment of marriage or other commitments. And in so far as honesty and concern for the other is present in a friendship, significant therapy can happen there as well even if it is not intended. Our own civic culture would prefer to keep therapeutic relationships sealed off from friendship. I can see where emotional entanglements might adversely affect psychotherapy and yet I wonder about the effectiveness of therapy if there is not some basis for friendship there.

I understand that the Irish at one time put great emphasis on spiritual companioning as a way to provide for good, healthy guidance and that the basis for this companioning was friendship. In my opinion, the present cultural tendency to try to get people to separate their friendships from professional relationships is not always or necessarily a good idea and over-compartmentalizes life. Friendship is so necessary for a full and healthy life that people should be free to embrace it wherever it may be found and not be unduly constrained by law or custom.

Of course there are professional relationships, as between therapist and client that are so potentially charged with affect, that one must be quite cautious and guarded in this regard, and make sure that this "container" is always safeguarded. In this and many other professional relationships, there is simply no room for other kinds of friendships or romances.

Augustine

Augustine in his Confessions describes himself as someone who basically experienced God's absence. He stresses interiority for both himself and others and this interiority requires recollection (Fr. Robert Dodaro in his presentation on the Confessions, Rome, Jan. 30, 2012). Augustine is "recollecting" and holding his experiences, both good and bad, in his mind very consciously, and, at least in part, as a way to encourage his readers to do the same. He wants people to know and appreciate that God can be found in absence as well as in ecstasy. Augustine is "stretching" us by his contrasts (God most just and most merciful, most hidden and most present, unchangeable and all-changing, numquam novus, numquam vetus, never new, never old; Confessions 1.4.4) so that we conclude that the divine is beyond human understanding. Or, as Fr. Dodaro put it, Augustine wants us to live in uncertainty: we must not domesticate God. We will not understand God but we must try to think of and speak of God anyway. As a Platonist one can conjure up some image but God is not the image.

Augustine's Confessions

Augustine was hoping to inspire his hearers and readers to do what he was doing in the Confessions, which is to reveal one's deepest aspirations and even one's faults. So a good reflection for contemporary people, especially for those who profess to be in an Augustinian tradition, is: how willing am I to (at least to some extent and appropriately) be open and honest even about my failures? Is there not something in modern culture that either militates against this or goes to the other extreme of bearing all? Again, I would suggest that the via media rule is a good one here: to be at least somewhat revelatory in the context of one's community, more so when among close friends, and completely so with a trusted confessor or confidant. Augustine experienced "confessing" as something very salutary and healthy, and he was anxious that others share this experience as well for the good of their souls. Are we willing to accept his invitation?

Patristics and Depth Psychology

Several years ago I decided to attend a ten-week course on Patristics offered by the Jung Institute of Los Angeles. (I was at the time doing an internship there as a psychotherapist and considering becoming a Jungian analyst). The presenter was Dr. Edward Edinger. As it turned out I learned, among other things, that for Jung and Jungian analytical training and education, studying Patristics and particularly the writings of St. Augustine, are of paramount importance. Many currents of thought influenced Jung: Taoism, all the world's Alchemical systems, Quantum scientific theories, Platonism, the great world religious systems, and much more. But he had a special fondness for St. Augustine that went beyond intellectual curiosity. I think this historical personage fascinated Jung because though Augustine, as Jung, was quite the intellectual, Augustine was also a man of great sensitivity and passion, one who lived even more out of his feeling function than that of logical thinking, though he was good at both. Jung, as he himself continually stressed, was not concerned so much with theology, but rather with seeing theological concepts, doctrines and dogmas, in their metaphorical meanings as ways to describe psychological phenomena.

Fr. Dodaro, in a personal communication, mentioned that in all likelihood Augustine came to read and identify with Platonic thought mostly through Latin translations by way of Cicero. He also became familiar with Plotinus through Latin manuscripts, though later in life Augustine did have some access to Greek texts.

Jung was fluent in Greek and could read the works of Plato in their original forms. He also shared Augustine's felt insight on the need for God's grace, especially in confronting those human weaknesses we usually describe as addictions. It was Jung who got the Twelve-step originators of Alcoholics Anonymous to include the idea of seeking God, as one understands Him. Again, though, Jung was not a theologian and did not want to seem to be one. However, he was a proponent of another Twelve-step notion: to admit one's powerlessness over "addictions" and thus to come to rely on a power beyond oneself; I imagine Jung must be speaking here of grace. To broaden this concept, people often have experiences of powerlessness when confronted with certain situations beyond their control. To admit one's powerlessness in the light of such situations is actually empowering. I think Augustine would say that grace is here working all along. The person comes to admit powerlessness because moved by grace to do so and then the humility that ensues helps bring about, again as by grace, an experience of salvation in the situation.

Vocatus aut non vocatus, Deus adeirit, Jung had inscribed over the main entrance to his home in Kusnacht, Switzerland: Called or not called, God will be there. Maybe a better translation would be something like: Whether you ask God to be with you or not, God's going to be there (whether you like it or not). Though dealing to a large extent as a psychotherapist with his clients' inner and very unique and personal worlds, Jung valued objectivity. When asked whether he believed in God, his response was, "I don't need to believe, I know." He may be skating here on the edge of a certain Gnosticism, but I think his emphasis on experience combined with his conviction of God's objective existence, indicates a healthy balance. In fact, I would say it's an Augustinian stance. Of course, Augustine was a person of profound faith and a committed Catholic Christian. Jung could not bring himself to such a place; his childhood and youth experiences in the Swiss Reformed religion of his clergyman father were too negative for that. Yet Jung too was deeply religious in a most broad and comprehensive sense, and did identify as a Christian.

The Problem of Evil

Augustine came up with a way of speaking about evil that has influenced theology ever since: that evil is the absence of the good. He was speaking as a theologian and within what's called "ontology," a branch of metaphysics that aims at understanding how things are objectively in themselves. Jung never much liked Augustine's observations on evil. For Jung evil was very substantial. Jung claimed not to want to speak theologically or metaphysically, but rather as a psychologist. I think here he is speaking out of psychological phenomenology. He's speaking of evil as something he has come in contact with, as something that has impinged upon him personally and which he has also observed objectively in war and in the holocaust. I imagine they both could be right since they are coming at the problem from different starting places and using different categories of meaning. Whatever the case, one would do well not to be overly optimistic about human nature, since, even though objectively grace is ever present and seeking to influence and move us along right paths, we are free to ignore it and to shape a destiny that denies or seeks to disregard it.

Augustinian Spirituality

One would probably imagine Augustinian Spirituality as essentially Catholic Christian. Yet I think it within the realm of possibility that other Christian traditions and even non-Christian belief systems could make use of this model as a way to live out their own spirituality. What I mean essentially is that a group of persons from whatever tradition might decide to form a community of like-minded persons, dedicate themselves to community, engage in both a common prayer life and in pastoral work of some kind, collectively or individually, be willing to challenge each other toward growth in the spiritual life and have a commitment to the construction of a better world and an end to violence. I would even imagine that there are such groups in the world in different non-Christian religions, and I hope those of us who are explicitly of the Catholic faith can encourage such spiritual paths.

I wonder if even some people who are professedly Marxist might not benefit from making use of some form of Augustinian spirituality. One might even critique religious and political/economic ideologies from this standpoint: can one really be committed to social justice issues without some spirituality to support one? And aside from economic issues, do ideologies go into decline precisely because of lack of a vibrant spirituality? And, on the other hand, has contemporary Christianity gone into a decline due to a turning away from the gospel imperative to put the most alienated and the least among us, first?

Iconography http://en.wikipedia.org/wiki/Iconography

This is, like vocations, another instance of paying attention to "what is wanted." If one is open to "the other," the icon itself will communicate with you as you create. The icon will take on something of the artist. Icons come out of Incarnation theology. The closer you get to the image of the icon the closer it gets to you. Here again archetypes are bustling around. The icon will also reflect some mistakes or imperfections of the artist like anything else one produces.

One does not paint but rather write an icon. In an Orthodox church one is surrounded by imagery, by the Word of God; one is contained. When you enter the church you see Veronica's veil above the entrance. Veronica means true image, the true icona of Christ. Icons were the jumpstart of the Renaissance: from places of origin to Constantinople, Ravenna, Russia, Serbia, Ukraine, etc. In Egypt and Ethiopia we have the Coptic style, in Greece and its environs, the Greek style, then the Russian. Icons grew out of the monastic spirituality of the East. In icons some of the halo is outside the sacred space (symbolic). One prays to the saint being depicted while making an icon. One tries to let go and not be in charge and relies on interior movements. And, as mentioned in the previous paragraph, the artist is always asking what is wanted. An icon will also tend to take on the characteristics of its creator.

An icon takes on a spirit that other works of art do not, like a Fra Angelico who was a close kin to the icon makers. So accompanying one's creation with a prayerful spirit is of the essence. The angels are important in iconography and on the iconostasis as God's messengers. I wonder to what extent the angels correspond to certain archetypal forces. There's lots of color symbolism as well in iconography, a color for divinity and a color for humanity as well. After the iconoclastic movement, the resolution was that one could make and venerate icons because of the Incarnation.

Prior to applying gold leaf to the halo of the saint, one breathes on the substance of the canvas before each application three times (as God breathed on the clay), for Father, Son, and Spirit and then the gold will stick. The exposed hand and face are covered over with a dark substance such that later on and bit by bit the light might come from within the icon, like light out of darkness. Divine darkness precedes divine light. Chaos came before order.

St. Luke is considered the patron of artists. Not that he necessarily painted, but he writes as a painter, describing scenes like the Annunciation with great detail. There are many traditions that Luke painted this or that icon. Not that it makes any difference. Also, the only halo with a cross in it is that of Christ. Luke tells us the stories of the infant Jesus and describes in detail many of the women in Jesus' life.

Colors in icons: the higher one goes in the color line the more importance is given the figure. Purple would be the highest. Green symbolizes the humanity of Jesus and red his divinity. Often Christ or a saint is pictured holding the book of scriptures, sometimes open, sometimes closed.

The icon remembers its prototype: the person in whose image it is portrayed. It's important to pray the icon to completion and ask the Spirit to bless the work. Icons will reflect something of the imperfections of the creator.

Sometimes icons of Mary have three stars on them; that means Mary was a virgin before, during and after Jesus' birth. Icon as a word means image. Icons are very personal and in a way become what the viewer is looking for. In some icons the eyes are red, symbolizing the fiery eyes of God. The eight-pointed star: seven days of creation, then the day that is eternal. A Christ-child losing one of its sandals symbolizes the child trying to get away from something.

10

PLANNING

In this chapter I offer some suggestions about planning, both personal and for work. I show how imagination is very important in planning and how certain forms of anxiety and other complexes militate against good planning. Finally, I describe a type of planning called "archetypal interactionist."

A technique

From a Christian perspective, keeping Quantum thought uppermost in one's mind would be equivalent to having the "Reign of God" as one's major goal. And that's why I include some reflections on planning in this paper: in order to communicate the importance of always keeping in mind the main goal which, however phrased, would include the notion of living in cooperation with Self and seeking the construction of a more just and loving world by giving preferential attention to the most marginated and alienated, and seeking to be as conscious as possible of the workings of God's grace in you and through you and even in spite of you.

Planning is an area for which I feel a certain affinity. I find it helpful to write down yearly or so a formulation of my basic values, which would be values held sacred by the Quantum approach and which are congruent with Jesus' parables and sayings on the Reign of God. From one's personally felt values you can formulate a short vision statement and then concretize that into a personal mission statement and then list four or five goals you want to work on. Then make a list of your many roles (like mother, teacher, husband, friend, etc.), and with each role write down one or two actions you want to accomplish which will help you get to your goals, mission and vision. That's a basic outline of a method described in detail in a book by Steven R. Covey on planning (The Seven Habits of Highly Effective People).

I would add to that a technique I learned from the Better World Movement which is that you ask this question of each goal in order to formulate your action statements: *what obstacles stand in the way of my accomplishing this goal or objective?* Then you might need to ask the same question of yourself as regards your contemplated actions so as to become more and more concrete. I find this method really valuable in keeping me grounded and clear about my life's direction. And probably no one else is going to do personal planning for you so it is better to assume that responsibility and just do it;

otherwise you might be very idealistic but never reach your goals.

What is often left out of planning, both personal and group, is the idea that people who are by nature more feeling and more intuitive-oriented, need to bring these functions into the planning process. Thinking and sensate types, as valuable as their contributions are, ought not have exclusive rights in planning. The feeling person would rightly be asking, "How does this direction or goal *feel* to me, and what might be the possible impacts and consequences of my decisions? And the intuitive would be concerned about imaging the future, and about getting under the "manifest" and seeing into archetypal fields and cores. In combination, an intuitive feeler would be very sensitive to "fields" projected by directions and goals, and would need to take any reactions to fields very seriously and as a basis for pursuing or for rejecting or modifying some direction or goal.

Pastoral Planning

There is a Quantum approach to group planning. This could take many forms, but it would essentially include aiming at involving all interested parties in the planning process and in seeking that all involved gain a holistic sense of the enterprise and buy into its mission, aims and goals. People more likely buy into the aims of an enterprise if they have participated in its planning. And this would include getting the participants (or some representative group making up an organizational Ego) to surface the major archetypes out of which they operate so they can plan around their strengths, and their shadow archetypes, and so they can become conscious of where obstacles lie. This can be done pastorally as in a parish and can be so organized as to involve all staff and parishioners who may wish to participate. This could also be a way, albeit a small way, to move church structures away from the patriarchal, patron model toward a more democratic, quantum one. And if there is an Augustinian-inspired community there and visible to the parishioners, that could prove very inspiring to them as a model. However, if the Augustinian community is mostly individualistic that could prove to be an obstacle to parish planning.

Imaging and Imagining

When I can picture in my mind some goal I'm aiming for and when I can so play with the images that I begin imagining I'm already there, I find it easier to move toward that particular goal. I suggest this practice both in personal and in other kinds of planning such as in the pastoral field. I believe that if a person charged with planning can motivate constituents toward picturing where they want to go, even lead them in a sort of imagery fantasy, they will be more creative and more committed to the projected goal. This would be a kind of "active imagination" on a group scale. Many archetypes might get activated in a group planning effort, especially the archetype of the Seeker/Explorer.

It might be a good idea for someone who is interested in the experiencing and application of archetypal theory to even intentionally "plan" on developing particular archetypes, or on going back to re-experience archetypes from one's past.

Anxiety and the Puer Complex

"Puer" means boy and "Puella" means girl. These are Latin terms used to denote a rather common personality disorder that is characterized by lack of commitment and stability and a tendency to think change and movement will bring about some imagined state of happiness and fulfillment. At times this disorder is closely linked to deeply felt and often unconscious anxiety that stems from early childhood abandonment either real or imagined. The best response on the part of others to behaviors coming out of such primitive and regressive "puer" and "puella" basic archetypal phenomena, is compassion, stability and patience and refusal to get drawn into the anxiety, excitement and drama which often accompany such "attacks" or "possessions."

12-step programs can be very helpful to people experiencing these sorts of moods since the predictable structure of the meetings and the guidance offered for working the steps and the presence of sponsors, provide a "space" of containment and security which gets to the root of the problem. Also, often lurking behind addictions of various kinds or even behind an addictive personality is the "puella" or "puer" syndrome. For some people, once addictions have been substantially dealt with, psychotherapy could prove of benefit for this disorder. "Puer" and "puella" figures might be personified in one's dreams and these would be fruitful material for psychological work in this area. However, addictions must be dealt with first prior to any depth psychological work.

The reason I have included the above description in this section on Planning is because such disorders tend to pose an obstacle to planning and, of course, they also prevent genuine interaction between people. When you interact with a person caught up in a "puer" or "puella" complex you are really interacting with the complex, not the real person. If you've ever felt overwhelming anxiety then you can empathize with how such a person is feeling. They are in a state of panic and feel like they might explode. They have a tremendous desire to get from "here" to "there" with no real objective need for such movement. It helps no one to take a condemnatory or judgmental stance Vis-a-vis such people. After all, they might well be you or I.

Archetypal Interactionist Planning

This style of planning would be more circular than linear because as the planner or group of planners gains more insight into the array of archetypal fields affecting them, their planning will change accordingly. Basically, this adaptation is necessary because the planning team will likely see a need to plan in order to affect the archetypal fields they see emerging, maybe even to the extent of devising interventions so as to disrupt or move some field pattern.

This is a kind of planning which takes into account archetypal pattern analysis. What are the planners seeing in their organization? What kinds of fields are there? Do those fields need to be affirmed and continued as part of the organization or do they need "interference" and intervention given the mission, aims and goals of the organization?

Sometimes in planning, a person can get a sense of what "reality" wants and so correspond one's planning accordingly. This is a clear example of how the future can help construct the plan for the present. This is a "wisdom" planning. You see where things want to go and how they want to get there, not in a fatalistic sense, but as "vocation" and fate and as the way life wants to move. So the best question to ask is: "What wants to happen." Rather than "What do *I* want to happen." This is a kind of practical way of taking grace into account and stressing its importance.

Another aspect of planning, especially life planning, is being open not just to indications based on reason but those that also come from one's organism. So one asks oneself: "As I ponder some possible scenarios, what do I feel in my body? Which scenarios give me a feeling of stress and which give me a sense of peace and relaxation?" This way one's physical being becomes a sounding board for or against certain directions or decisions. Of course you'd have to blend this in with what your mind is indicating too, and what prayerful discernment reveals.

Self

And once you start asking the question "what is wanted?" you are moving into the orbit of Self, that mysterious archetype of the human psyche that feels somehow divine and that embraces the totality of a person and an organization. Here one must tread very carefully and respectfully, because the attitude a person or an organization takes toward its very Self will be the same one mirrored back. What Self wants, just as Shadow and Animus/Anima, is relationship. One must not ignore, or be indifferent, or try to dominate, or let oneself be dominated either. And as there are people in one's world who carry the Shadow, and Animus/Anima, so there are people who image Self. How you relate with them will help determine how you relate with Self within.

The greatest challenge for all of us is to do what we can to get ego out of the way so that the voice of Self, which tends to speak in whispers, can be heard. To be in touch with one's persona, shadow, anima/animus, and one's other archetypes, and the Self seems like an impossible task, but it can be done, I think the main thing to keep in mind in this work is to incessantly work for consciousness. It is this dialogical attitude one has toward the unconscious that causes the unconscious and its contents to take a person seriously and to respond with the same degree of respect it is receiving. And of course there is a continual, reciprocal relationship within any person between how they are treating flesh and blood people "out there" and how one's inner figures will treat oneself. The inner and the outer are not really two distinct worlds, but two sides of the same coin.

I want to stress once again the central place of prayer for both individuals and for those who make up organizational egos. Archetypal fields, both for good and for ill, surround us all the time. I believe we can affect these fields, make them more positive, or even neutralize the negative ones, by our attitudes and prayers. And the more specific a person or an organization can be in praying for its wholeness and integrity, the better. Getting people to name the objects of their prayers, and especially concentrating on having good connections with one's Self, cannot help but be beneficial for a person and an organization.

From a Quantum perspective, there's more out there than meets the eye. There's a huge web tying all things together of which we are a part and which responds to our intentionality. And God's grace is permeating that web.

11

OPUS CONTRA NATURAM

This chapter is a write-up of how people may be living out the archetypes mentioned in the paragraphs that follow. The intent in identifying these archetypes and their fields is not primarily academic, but, rather, is meant to assist us individually and as groups to more consciously move toward greater personal and collective development and integration.

This expression, "opus contra naturam," is Latin for "the work against nature." It comes from Medieval European Alchemy and is frequently quoted by Jung in his writings. What this refers to is that once people know more or less what their basic individual nature is like, they can deliberately begin to "go against it" in the sense of trying to more consciously develop opposites, or the "shadow." "Opus" or "Work" as used in this expression, while directly referring to alchemical processes, can be understood to mean psychological work; that might be an individual's work on her or himself or work with another in a psychotherapeutic or other counseling setting, or even education or staff development. The concept is more easily understood from concrete examples. Suppose a person has achieved a certain level of professional and work development, but is beginning to feel a malaise and unease in living. With some knowledge of Jungian archetypal and developmental psychology, this person might come to the conclusion that he or she has been overdoing things ego-wise, and that now is the time for better Self emphasis. " Self " as used here means the inner presence of the numinous or the divine. If this person is fortunate, there will come along an experience, either consciously or unconsciously, of the Self. Sometimes a "numinous" experience occurs in a dream and at other times through nature or in some other conscious way.

Another way to look at this area of "opus contra naturam" is to imagine that whatever is a strength is in "consciousness" and whatever is undeveloped is "unconscious." So, often the word "shadow" is used on an individual basis to refer to whatever is not available to consciousness. In this sense, each person's consciousness and unconsciousness is different from all others, even given the objectivity of conscious and unconscious archetypes in general.

Bases for Profiling

Getting a bit more specific, each person's ego development goes along these lines as well, with usually one of the following as a person's strong area, one as weak or in the "shadow," and two, more or less available: Parent (authority, guiding, ruler, directive, etc.), with its opposite, Child ("puer," "puella", companion, innocent, everyperson, brotherhood, sisterhood, etc.), Warrior (fighter, debater, resister, challenger, etc.), and its opposite Wise Person (student, philosopher, magician, academic, etc.).

Psychological Typology is also archetypal. Each letter used represents an archetypal field. So E/I (extravert/introvert), S/N (sensate/intuitive), T/F (thinker/feeler), and J/P (judger/perceiver). And certain combinations of these archetypes produce other fields. "Fields" as used here is similar to "energy." Sometimes this energy is quite palpable and conscious to a person and sometimes one is simply not aware of its presence or how one is being affected by it. This area is described in greater detail in the chapter on Depth Psychology. The SP is motivated by Action, the NF by the Search for Meaning, the SJ by Belonging and the NT by Precision, and these motivators are experienced as fields, sometimes so strongly that a person feels impelled or even possessed by it.

There is a tendency right now in Catholic parish congregations for some people to classify members according to the categories of conservative/progressive. I am of the view that people don't usually decide to be either one or the other, but rather it is their basic propensity toward either a Newtonian or a Quantum worldview that determines this. And usually some combinations of the psychological functions are also indicative of probable conservative or progressive leanings. For example, I imagine the combinations of SJ and NT may well indicate a more conservative mentality and an NF and SP a more progressive one. I would posit this since SJ results in a person who is very enamored of institutions and an NT combination results in a person who sees most value in precision and exactness. The NF person is very future and possibility oriented and the SP is most motivated by the desire to stay continually active. If this is true, then there's a fairly even percentage of people in both categories of Newton and Quantum (SJ's are 38%, NT's are 12%, SP's are 38% and NF's are 12% of the population). This is purely speculative on my part. And of course most people are a blend of both progressive and conservative tendencies, as circumstances warrant. I am suggesting general tendencies, not absolute black and white divisions based on typology. Nor am I suggesting that it is somehow morally superior to be either Quantum or Newtonian oriented.

Getting more specific still, and using as previously the archetypes identified by Corlett & Pearson in Mapping the Organizational Psyche and by Pearson in Awakening the Heroes Within, we have: (Ego development) Innocent (Everyperson), Orphan, Warrior and Caregiver; (Soul development) Seeker, Destroyer, Lover, and Creator; (Self development) Ruler, Sage, Magician and Jester. The meaning of the archetypes of the psyche as well as of those mentioned in the preceding paragraphs, have already been defined in previous chapters of this book. At this point I will only offer definitions of those developmental archetypes from Pearson.

"Archetypes provide the deep structure for human motivation and meaning. When we encounter them in art, literature, sacred texts, and advertising—or in individuals or groups—they evoke deep feeling within us. These imprints, which are hardwired in our psyches, were projected outward by the ancients onto images of gods and goddesses. Plato disconnected these from religion, seeing them in philosophical terms as "elemental forms." Twentieth-century psychiatrist C.G. Jung called them "archetypes."

Corlett and Pearson collect these archetypes in three categories, each one holding four archetypes: {*I highly recommend purchasing their books as they are most practical*}.

Preparation: Archetypes of the Family (Innocent, Orphan, Caregiver and Warrior). These archetypes provide a person with foundational energies moving one toward independence from the family.

The Journey: Archetypes of Transformation and Change (Explorer, Destroyer, Lover and Creator). These archetypes help establish a person as a productive member of society and culture.

The Return: Archetypes of the Royal Court (Ruler, Magician, Sage and Jester). These archetypal energies deepen a person and enable one to more clearly discern and use those talents and abilities that will be both personally and socially productive.

Developmental Archetypes
(This is a term I use for these archetypes because it is descriptive of their functions).

Innocent: Seeing the world as basically trustworthy and good.
Orphan: Realizing that all is not as it should be, but bad things happen too.
Warrior: Learning to stand up for oneself and for the more vulnerable.
Caregiver: Reaching out to others with concern and compassion.
Seeker: Looking for and trying out new ways of doing things.
Lover: Recognizing one's attractions and feeling love, affection and commitment.
Destroyer: Being willing to let go of attitudes and possessions that no longer serve.
Creator: Coming up with new and original ways of confronting one's world.
Ruler: Becoming responsible for oneself and one's basic values.
Magician: Being able to make inner changes that affect outer events.
Sage: Seeing things more clearly and profoundly beyond the manifest.
Jester: Appreciating ambivalence and seeing humor in life's heaviness.

These developmental archetypes are present in both people individually and in their groups and organizations. The underlying idea in discovering these and working with them so as to manifest as much as possible their positive side, is to relate with them consciously as potential helpmates on life's journey. Not being conscious of how they operate in one's life or organization means risking the possibility of these energies possessing a person and leading one blindly down paths one has not necessarily chosen.

And just as individuals will benefit from knowing about their psychological makeup in terms of functions and attitudes and other archetypes, so will organizations. In fact, if one wants to deeply uncover the inner workings of some group or organization, all these categories we usually think of as pertaining to individuals can also be very helpful in dealing with various enterprises, both large and small. The first step in organizing a depth analysis of an organization is deciding on who will comprise the organizational ego: you would need a large enough group of people so that all the "faces" (People, Learning, Results and Stabilizing), of the organization are adequately represented but not so many individuals that the group becomes unwieldy (see also Chap. 6, Organizational Development).

So in analyzing some organization, try to determine if it's more extravert or introvert, if it tends to be more judgmental or more perceptive, if it's more intuitive or sensate, feeling or thinking. And see if you can ascribe a type to it as you would to an individual. And what is the organization's temperament? Also, can you determine the organization's balance of anima and animus energy? Then, finally, once you have established a typological description of the organization, what would be your recommendations to move the organization toward greater wholeness? Just as in individuals, the suggestions you will make to complement the conscious structure of the organization will be "opus contra naturam." That is to say, the undeveloped attitudes and functions are out of the unconscious, and so not "natural" to the conscious organization. But they can nevertheless be developed deliberately and consciously, although with difficulty and struggle.

The same principle holds true for the developmental archetypes: determine which "faces" of the organization are most consciously operative and therefore which of the archetypes, then figure out how to get the more unconscious ones brought to consciousness so as to produce a more holistic and better functioning organization.

Quite likely, in doing this kind of qualitative depth analysis, the temptation will be to try to quantify the results and set up some specific measurable criteria for success. That would be a mistake. Any organization or business already has or can have at its disposal any number of quantitative measurements, but a depth analysis is a different approach to organizational health and development and is Quantum, not quantitative, which implies indeterminacy with a concentration on patterns and fields and their respective archetypes. I believe the best methodology to use when dealing with the Quantum world is that of Symbolic Interactionism described herein in Chapter 2.

Just as people (when doing well) love themselves and hope for the best for themselves and others, so organizations can hope for their best and the ego of the organization can work to so uncover its strengths and weaknesses, that it can love the organization into health and wholeness. And it seems to me that prayer is efficacious for both people and organizations. If you love someone or some organization, you will hold them in your heart and pray for them and ask the divine to bless and heal them. Inner work and organizational work are holy works of healing and should not be left up to Newton alone.

"Every archetype displays very specific behaviors when it overheats or freezes -that is when it operates with either too much energy, or not enough energy. In the Overheated state, the character launches into excessive expression. In their Frozen state the individual acts as if they are incapable of accessing the traits of the archetype, justifying their inaction with a multitude of reasons. Neither state is helpful for either ourselves or those around us." Pad, 32-35 (2011-07-01).

The above is from a very short booklet. I think the concept of overheating or freezing of archetypes might be helpful to people who find benefit in doing self-analysis to see how their archetypes are fairing. That once in a while either overheating or freezing of archetypes should take place I don't think is unusual. To become aware of *when* it happens and perhaps *why* it happens could be quite valuable. Sometimes one's physical condition of illness or tiredness could have a great deal to do with this, esp. the freezing part. In terms of this chapter, "Opus Contra Naturam," one can be summoned to either put more energy into some archetype or siphon energy off depending on whether the archetype is too heated or too cooled. This process also can be seen as "opus contra naturam" in that when one naturally feels caught in some extreme of an archetype, one can go against that and choose to move toward the opposite. The ideal is, of course, Augustine's *via media*.

12

PLATO, AUGUSTINE, AND JUNG

In this chapter I contrast St. Augustine and Carl Jung, show the central thrust of Augustine's spirituality and something of the early history of the Order and its emerging spirituality.

Plato

"In 427 B.C., the Ancient Greek city-state of Athens was flourishing. Approximately 80 years earlier, the Athenians had formed the first self-representative democracy in history, the Peloponnesian War against Sparta had only just started, and Socrates was only beginning to lay the foundation of what would become Western philosophy. That year Plato was born to a wealthy family: with an uncle who was close friends with Socrates, Plato was seemingly destined to become a philosopher. By the end of his life, Plato had indeed become the foremost philosopher of his time, and perhaps the most famous philosopher in Western history." From Intro. to Timaeus, Kindle, 2011.

Plato describes his cave metaphor at the beginning of Book 7 of the Republic. In essence he is saying that "we see dimly now, as in a cloudy mirror." As St. Paul would say several centuries later. Plato is saying that we live in a world of appearances but the really real is beyond us and ordinarily that we are not perceptive of this world. I think Plato's insight was that the real world beyond the visible is the Quantum one. So when I say "Plato" here, I mean mainly the idea that there's more to reality than meets the eye (using the famous shadows on the cave wall analogy or metaphor).

Augustine

By "Augustine," I mean that one of these realities we don't see very well is God's grace. And by "Jung," I mean the idea that the more conscious one can become of those unseen realities, the better off one is. Of course, Plato, Augustine and Jung aren't just metaphors but real, historical characters; and each one with a huge volume of writings. Although Plato is the instigator of the ideas about reality that later would have so much influence on Augustine (mainly by way of Latin translations and to some extent as refracted through Cicero and then the Neo-Platonists), Augustine and Jung (d. 1961) are the main protagonists. I have already treated extensively of Jung and the Jungians and their relevant ideas in previous chapters. In this one I will concentrate mostly on

Augustine (d. 430) while also doing some comparing and contrasting of the two.

Jung

To get right to the point: Jung's concentration is on coming to greater consciousness (the process of individuation), and, in particular, coming to greater consciousness of what is going on when one is experiencing inner turmoil or some confrontation with the unconscious. Jung's method is psychotherapy, and then when sufficiently along the road toward individuation, to have the client engage in what he called *active imagination* (cfr. Johnson, & Stein). Augustine certainly wants us to be more conscious too. But Augustine is more concerned with a deeper, even more hidden reality than what came to be called the unconscious: God's grace. And the method, or context for Augustine in living a graced life is *community*, and in particular, community as described and envisioned by the Acts of the Apostles. So the monks or friars are to practice the sharing of goods and live together in harmony.

With Jung it's as though one must become completely responsible for achieving consciousness; with Augustine this quest is not just one of human effort; it is accompanied always by and under the influence of grace. (jn.15.5) " I am the vine, ye are the branches: He that abideth in me, and I in him, the same bringeth forth much fruit: for without me ye can do nothing." Kindle Bible (KJV). Maybe Jung experienced and believed this too, but if so, he didn't say. He did use the expression when speaking of the healing power of the *Transcendent Function*, "as if by grace," but then denied that he was speaking theologically (*The Ego-Self Axis).*

So in constructing a spirituality or discovering the outlines of a spirituality that would be appealing to people of our time, I would suggest that using Jung's basic mapping of the soul (summed up in this paper), and knowing that one will with some frequency be pushed toward a confrontation with the unconscious; that, while this happens, one will also remember that God's grace is always present and that suffering can be alleviated and balance restored by confessing powerlessness and experiencing grace. This is essentially a Jungian/Augustinian synthesis.

Reading the Confessions and the Sermons of St. Augustine are a great help in this regard, as are his Commentaries on the Psalms. Augustine went through a period of turmoil when he was involved with the Manicheans. This religious system rejected the Old Testament and even some of the New. Their questions about O.T. behavior, like polygamy, perturbed Augustine greatly. He was also pushed to the edge just prior to his baptism due to having to split from his female companion, the mother of his son, Adeodatus. He was not allowed under Roman law to marry her due to class differences. So how did he resolve these confusions and sufferings? He first experienced God's grace by his own testimony (Cassiciacum) and in the light of this grace he was able to see the fallacy of the Manicheans and felt healed in his personal life. Jung (who had between 1912 and 1918 more or less a similar kind of mental and emotional breakdown, though for different reasons), would say that Augustine admitted his powerlessness.

There's a word in Jungian theory, "enantiodromia," which is probably not employed very much by anyone. But it is descriptive of both Augustine and Jung as they endure their tests by fire. What it refers to is the tendency many people have at times to swing between two extremes when "what is wanted" is for one to embrace the middle ground. So someone is at one moment a pious "Donatist" and the next moment a worldly "Pelagian." If one could just stick to the middle! Eventually, after his crisis reached its apogee at Cassiciacum and Augustine became a Catholic Christian, that's what he did. I think Jung lived mostly in the *via media* also, though certainly as an introvert. As an imperial bishop Augustine could not afford to live very introvertedly, though he was certainly introspective. Rather, he had to live his life as a public person, sometimes as bishop, sometimes as judge. Jung could afford to be a man of leisure with just a few clients and with plenty of time to do research and to write. Augustine, I imagine, was busy from sunrise to sunset, if not about church business then as a magistrate. Christians had the option of either taking their cases to a civil court or to the local bishop. Augustine had a reputation for honesty and integrity, so of course people preferred him to the civil magistrates.

I find it interesting here to contrast our two protagonists: Jung's breakdown is precipitated by his disillusionment and then complete severing of ties with his mentor and father figure, Sigmund Freud. Augustine becomes, finally, completely disgusted with the Manicheans after waiting with great anticipation for the coming of the Manichean bishop, Faustus. As with other groups of Gnostics, the core of Manichean theology was the "secret" which only the completely initiated and purified would be taught. Augustine felt he was ready for this. Then Faustus arrives and tells Augustine that there really isn't any secret knowledge after all. Eventually Augustine will learn that the concept of an elite group with secret knowledge is totally repugnant to Catholic Christianity.

Even Augustine's reading of Neo-Platonic texts contributed eventually to his confusion and inner turmoil. The purpose of Neo-Platonism was to re-read Plato but to do so in the light of many of the philosophical movements of the time (like Stoicism, Pythagoreanism, Cynicism). They didn't call themselves Neo-Platonists, but just Philosophers. Augustine found much common ground between the Neo-Platonists and Catholic Christianity, an important piece of this is in the Prologue of the Gospel of John.

How did God's grace work in Augustine? He himself concluded that it was through other people and mostly through the rational religion of the Neo-Platonists. While Manicheans rejected the Incarnation, the Neo-Platonists talked of certain principles on the basis of which one can to an extent comprehend Christian doctrines, like the Trinity. Augustine didn't learn about Plato and Neo-Platonic thought just through his reading; he discussed texts and related matters with a group of friends and much of what he learned was by a kind of osmosis. Of course, the most important things: God's grace, Incarnation, Trinity, etc., Augustine came to learn as a Christian, specifically as a *Catholic* Christian. Re. the Incarnation: Augustine took the Pauline doctrine of *kenosis* and deduced that people need to apply this also to themselves; that if God would empty himself in Christ (Logos) and so embrace humility, so should we; in a way, by doing this we "incarnate" the other way, taking on something of the nature of God. Augustine "confesses" that he began his quest for wisdom after reading Cicero's Hortensius when he was about 18 or 19.

Augustine came to recognize his pride and his self-awareness prepared him for the grace of humility. Augustine says he experienced Christ as the way toward humility. Augustine moved out of the dualism of the Manicheans and beyond the rationalism of Neo-Platonism to the acceptance of living with ambiguity as a Catholic Christian. Retrospectively, Augustine saw that it was God who brought him to the Philosophers and then on to Catholic Christian Baptism.

I just re-read Augustine's account of his conversion experience in Book 8 of the Confessions. Certainly, I find the passage more moving when I *hear* it read. This time I noticed his allusion to the monk, Antony of Egypt, and I recalled a couple of years ago visiting an ancient monastery near Cairo that Antony had reputedly founded. I was very moved when our monk guide (we were three Catholic priests and had introduced ourselves as such to the Coptic priest monk), took us into their monastic chapel and then into the sanctuary behind the screen, and informed us that Mass has been celebrated here uninterruptedly since the third century. My reaction to that was similar to how I felt on visiting the old excavated baptistery under the Milan Duomo where Augustine was baptized toward the end of the fourth century. Sometimes I find these events overwhelming. And in my imagination I wonder if Augustine had a copy of Pachomius' monastic Rule and, if so, to what extent was he influenced by it when he was composing his own? And then, in 430, as he lay dying and his province was being overrun by the Vandals, and Patricius the young Britain or Celt as the case may be, was consecrated bishop and sent to Ireland, did he take with him both these rules of life and did they influence the development of Irish monasticism?

I know this is speculative, but such speculation offers a kind of big brush view of history that I like to keep in mind before getting caught up in the details.

When Augustine was bishop and writing his Confessions, the Donatists were the majority Christians. (I've read somewhere that when Augustine was first made bishop about half the population of the Roman province of Africa was pagan and about half was

Christian. Of the Christians, a slight majority were Donatists in and around Hippo. They believed that the bishops and clergy needed to be *seen* to be blameless of sin, that people need the illusion of a safe oasis. Jung would say that Donatism was possessed by *persona* and living in hypocrisy. So Augustine is writing his Confessions, the story of his own sinfulness and of his experience of grace in the context of a majority Christian group that did not want to hear what he was writing. Also, Augustine's polemic with Pelagius helps us understand better his insistence on the pervasive presence of grace in people's lives.

Donatism gets its name from the bishop Donatus who survived the Great Persecution under the emperor Diocletian (c. the first 12 years or so of the Fourth Century), a persecution that ended by Constantine's decree of religious toleration. This is a generation or so prior to Augustine's birth in 354. Many Christians, including priests and bishops, had succumbed to threats and denied the faith or handed over their sacred books to the authorities during the persecution. Donatus did not. He and his party (which included many who did in fact deny the faith at least in principle by bribing magistrates to give them safe-conduct vouchers without having to actually verbally deny Christ). But this was considered o.k. because it wasn't public knowledge; the mystique of holiness and faithfulness was maintained.

During the thirty-some years of Augustine's episcopacy, the Donatists and Catholics were very much at odds, even to the extent of attacking and killing each other, disrupting church services and burning down houses of worship. It's quite likely Monica herself was from a Donatist family though by the time Augustine came along she had become a fervent Catholic Christian. The basic area of strife and disagreement was over whether or not the sin of apostasy could be forgiven, and whether a bishop or priest who had fallen into apostasy but then repented, could validly celebrate the sacraments. The Donatists said *no*, the Catholics (including the Roman church), said *yes*, with certain stipulations depending on the gravity of the apostasy. Eventually, and while Augustine was bishop, he would use his authority to request a forced conversion and suppression of the Donatists. Those bishops who would come quietly into the fold were able to maintain their episcopal status; those who didn't were persecuted and imprisoned. Augustine didn't much like what he did. But even worse, the precedent he set in invoking the intervention of state power in religious matters would have terrible consequences in subsequent centuries, especially with the Albigencians of the late middle ages and the Inquisitions to follow.

It might occur to one that Donatism and Pelagianism haven't completely died out, that some Christians, even Catholic Christians, in their severity and fundamentalism keep incarnating this heresy, and many of us, quite frankly, in our quest for individuality and self-sufficiency, keep Pelagius alive. Augustine's doctrine on grace, in this respect, is a very healthy stance and it says as much about the human need for forgiveness and reconciliation as it does about God's magnanimity. An Augustinian spirituality, or even a more ecumenically and Quantum-universalist one would, I think, gladly embrace Augustine's position. Perhaps today the heresy of Pelagius is more difficult to deal with than that of Donatus, especially among European and North American Christians.

Augustine the theologian speculates on the doctrine of the Trinity and on the inner workings of God revealed in the New Testament as One yet somehow manifesting threeness. And making use in particular of the First Letter of John, he speaks of how the inner life of God is characterized by the mutuality of loving interactions, and how the love of the Father and the Son is maintained through the unifying power of the Spirit. Augustine the psychologist sees the Trinity as metaphoric for human interactions as well. Many centuries later Jung and the Jungians would apply this concept to people's interiority: that the Self is like the Father, containing all completeness within, and giving birth to the Ego. Then, once ego is overwhelmed by alienation and chaos, how the Transcendent Function (Holy Spirit) moves in on them and produces healing and restores the Ego-Self connection. And so it is that Augustine experienced himself as somehow having the life of the Trinity within himself, the Father loving the Son in him, and this mutual love being sealed by the power of the Spirit. And, by necessary extension, Augustine continuing this Trinitarian life by loving others as well, putting into practice the injunction, "How can you love God whom you cannot see if you don't love people whom you do see?"

And if God goes out of himself to love people, in particular "emptying" himself and becoming human in Christ, doesn't that call us also to a kind of emptying so that we too become humble by extending ourselves to others? This experience and insight of Augustine's on the life of the Trinity within becomes an essential part of Augustinian spirituality.

Augustine develops his theology of love mostly in his work <u>De Doctrina Cristiana</u>. To sum up his thoughts, Augustine is convinced that one is called to love God primarily in love for neighbor. The neighbor, of course, is not God. Yet experientially it's better not to separate things out, such that you bifurcate your love. As long as one is really, primarily, willing the good of the other, then loving that other, even if there is great enjoyment (frui) in the relationship, this love is "amor rectus." It is rightly ordered or righteous. And *amor rectus* has love of God as its ultimate aim even if that stays mostly on an unconscious level.

> Whoever, then, loves his neighbor aright, ought to urge upon him that he too should love God with his whole heart, and soul, and mind. For in this way, loving his neighbor as himself, a man turns the whole current of his love both for himself and his neighbor into the channel of the love of God, which suffers no stream to be drawn off from itself by whose diversion its own volume would be diminished. Augustine of Hippo, <u>On Christian Doctrine</u> (<u>De Doctrina Christiana</u>),

Kindle Edition, (pp. 23-24).

In his <u>Confessions,</u> Augustine describes in great detail his abjection and real despair over the death of a friend. He concludes that his love for this other was lacking in something; it was not "amor rectus." Probably it was a kind of codependent love wherein there is distortion and unhealthy projection going on. So not all love is truly *amor rectus*. But all *amor rectus* love is a binding love of the other and love of God together, *as though* they are one and the same.

Academic and Pastoral

Augustine's conversion was aided by his study of Neo-Platonism, but it was not this that converted him; it was God's Word. Augustine in his <u>Confessions</u> speaks of the insufficiencies of this philosophical system. There's a specific Christian streak in Augustine that cannot be ascribed to anything else. When one reads Augustine, one is witnessing Augustine making use of scripture continuously, but without citing texts usually. Scripture had become part of his vocabulary. And, though previously critical of St. Paul, the converted Augustine is now fond of Paul and his writings. So by way of imitation, how does God's Word take root in the rest of us as it did in Augustine? To some extent, words are used too much in our modern cultures; so much so that one doesn't pause sufficiently to contemplate them or let them sink in.

Augustine becomes more popular during times of great transition. People read him, esp. the <u>Confessions,</u> and they see themselves, even young college students. One reads Augustine not to become more like him, but to become more like Christ. Somehow the Word of God enabled him to articulate the movements of grace in his life. Augustine became like the texts of Scripture, because he loved these texts. Augustine lived in an oral culture, so it's not that he read scripture alone all that much, but he heard it read aloud and came to love what he heard. So Augustine came to see himself and his life as refracted through scripture, esp. through the writings of Paul; they jabbed at his memory and he recollected his own experience moved by the words of scripture.

The <u>Confessions</u> are Augustine's reflections on his experiences, esp. his experiences of grace and the apparent absence of grace. Reading him one can be readily moved to ponder one's own experiences and make some reflections on them. Book 10 is more a reflection on Augustine's present time as a bishop while he was writing. He's not writing as a personal purgation, but because he felt commanded to write them by God. What was he trying to accomplish? In that cultural context what he was doing was trying to get others to reflect on their lives and come to grips with them.

Augustine is not necessarily recounting pure facts: he is reflecting on his experiences as he remembers them; there is a recounting of past events to make them present in the "now." Augustine addresses God and wrote the <u>Confessions</u> as a conversation with God. He is aware that it was God who saved him, that it has been God's work, not his own. This raises similar questions in the reader: am I ascribing the initiative to God, or rather, am I wanting to take responsibility for my spiritual life?

Founding of the Order of Hermits of St. Augustine: an Emerging Spirituality

In the early history of the Order, studied not just for the sake of historical facts but also with an eye toward spirituality, there is a connection with Coptic monasticism in that Augustine, prior to the writing of the Rule, receives from his friend Pontitianus in Milan, prior even to his baptism, some reflections on early Egyptian monasticism, re. in particular Antony the Hermit. It's evident that Antony himself tended to move on seeking solitude when the crowds became too much for him, moving further into the desert wilderness. But at some point he stopped and came to grips with the reality that the common people too, and not just the hermit monks who wanted to share his insights about monasticism and the Christian life, wanted a share in his spirituality. So he opened up the monasteries to accommodate pilgrims. This accommodation was written into Pachomius' Rule with specific assignment given to one or more of the monks to take care of visitors and provide them hospitality. As incarnated by the early Augustinian movement of the 13th century, instead of taking the pilgrims into the monastery or hermitage, the friars were to go out and preach and minister to the people of the newly emerging city states. For a while these Augustinian Hermits had Episcopal authorization to preach and generally engage in ministry in and around the vicinity of their dwellings. Eventually they established houses in the cities and even took on responsibility for devotional churches and parishes as a basis for their ministry.

The several hermit groups who came together both initially in 1244 and then again in 1256 to make up the Order of Hermits of St. Augustine, already had some rules and regulations and in some cases even some specific constitutions to guide their common life. Of course, they were all buying into and even requesting the Rule of St. Augustine as the Charter of their religious life. Some of these groups had been living according to the Rule of St. Benedict. Now their common rule was to be officially that of St. Augustine. In the Constitutions which they formulated and which were ratified by 1290 (with some serious difficulties due to attempts to suppress the Augustinian Order and the Carmelites), it was clear that Community or common life was to be the glue that held them together, and the several provisions of the Constitutions were aimed at that. In terms of their emerging "spirituality," I think a good place to concentrate is on their practice of "Chapter of Faults." In my own experience as an Augustinian, we had a formalized ceremony like a Chapter of Faults, but originally the practice was fairly severe, with those brothers who wished accusing themselves publicly of certain faults, and sometimes others calling their reluctant brother friars to task for failing to admit what other knew they had done.

I think the *spirit* of this practice, as foreign as it seems to us today, can be healthy. And as a spirituality, it also conforms well to the Jungian psychoanalytic practice of baring one's soul to the analyst, coming thus to grips with what the Jungians call the *shadow* and shadow material, those elements of one's psyche/soul that tend to be more or less unconscious to one but need to be confronted consciously for the sake of individuation (read *holiness* in spirituality and *wholeness* in psychology). At times an analyst may be quite brutal in interpreting dream material or physical ailments (psychosomatic) to the client as a way to force "integration" (and thus conversion toward greater wholeness) of ego with Self (felt as the divine within). Now in religious life this practice has been relegated to sacramental confession and to the Chapter of Renewal. In the latter the friars are invited and encouraged to plan together to engage in spiritual practices like retreat days or common readings so as to facilitate personal and communal spiritual growth.

From the beginnings of the Augustinian Order in the 13th century, the importance of praying together the Hours of the Roman Breviary and assistance at both conventual and other celebrations of the Mass has been considered essential elements of its spirituality. Jung has a lengthy book on the Mass called Mysterium Transformationis. Part of his commentary includes the idea that for Eucharist to really be effective in one's life, one must truly believe that Jesus is present there in the forms of bread and wine. And he also stresses that the *mysterium* (sacrament) includes essentially the idea that just as the elements of bread and wine are transformed, so are those who partake of communion. Again Jung is saying that his comments are not to be taken theologically, that he is writing as a psychologist. I suppose we must take him at his word on this, but he is certainly skating close to the edge where theology and psychology meet. And one of his principal sources for Mysterium Transformationis is Augustine.

So prayer together, some sort of chapter of faults or renewal, Eucharist and growth in friendship, with everything pointing to the building up of community, has been and still is the core of Augustinian spirituality. Theologically underpinning all this and enabling it to happen in the face of great diversity, is God's grace. And those among us who would like to see a move toward a new paradigm as described previously in this paper, would do well to incarnate the spirit of this kind of community-centered spirituality in our own lives. Paradigms don't change until enough people are actually living some new, more desirable one.

"By working with your soul group, you begin to practice fellowship; you experience the awe-inspiring cooperation among all souls. Really understanding fellowship means you no longer hold yourself as separate from the world and are open to influencing and being influenced by everyone—whether they're close, far, friend, foe, physical, or nonphysical. It means you know how other people's growth makes conditions easier for you and how your clarity helps them. Fellowship is based on mutual, conscious communion. You are your brother and sister's keeper, and they are your keeper. You learn that as you tend to others' needs, your needs are magically attended to, as well. The idea is to treat the other person as though they are you and to imagine in great detail how you would feel living in their body, seeing life through their eyes. Then imagine others stepping into your shoes to do the same." Peirce, Penney, Frequency, Kindle Edition. (p. 250, 251).

There are many archetypal forces that interact when an Augustinian spirituality is being lived deeply: the focus the community members have on prayer and God's abiding grace brings them into touch collectively and individually with the archetype of the *Self*; an admission of the need for repentance from faults and sins committed gets them in touch with their respective individual and group *shadows*; introspection regarding tendencies to do things just for show helps bring about a confrontation with common and individual "*personas;*" recognition of power plays in the community can be a way to stir up reflection on and maybe some intentions regarding seeking a better balance of *yin* and *yang* energies; as community members come to know each other better from their many interactions, personal and communal, they may well come to a recognition that while holding many things in common, they are and will remain nonetheless, very different people with different mixes of *psychological functions and attitudes*.

One relationship and so archetypal interaction that takes place in people and which describes an Augustinian spirituality is this: the Transcendent Function (experienced *as though* the Holy Spirit) comes to each soul and heals the alienation that has occurred during the span of one's life by reuniting the Ego (experienced *as though* Christ, the Son), with the Self (experienced *as though* the Father). This interior archetypal interaction may result in some mystical experience or even feel quite natural to the individual. And you can see how this kind of description, a translation into archetypal entities, is both psychological and theological, both Jungian and Augustinian. My faith tells me that there really does take place in people this dynamic indwelling of the Trinity, and that it's not only a psychological, *as though* experience. Or it might be more accurate to say that the Trinity is always present to one but we only come to awareness of this once in a while.

And, as community members come to know each other progressively better, they will also be able to realistically comment on and offer suggestions about where they stand relative to the living out or not of the developmental archetypes (read also, virtues.) Another area contributing essentially to Augustinian spirituality is that of study, both individually and collectively. This kind of community interaction will also, hopefully, lead the members to realize that each person, being constructed quite differently and with unique *soul* needs and callings, needs to seek ministerial activity accordingly; the same shoe doesn't fit all. Psychologically put, "where is your bliss?" This notion doesn't have much to do with *ego* but it has everything to do with soul and Self. But this is in no way a disembodied spirituality. It has as a central goal the preferential option for the least among us, the most marginated and the most neglected. To embrace the contemplative side of this spirituality and ignore the social justice side, would be to run to "Donatus" and avoid "Pelagius." It would give traction to the Marxist critique of religion as being a kind of opiate.

The 1290 <u>Constitutions</u> have been revised several times over the centuries at General Church Councils and Order General Chapters as the *signs of the times* have necessitated. The latest revisions occurred in 2007. But the essence of the spirituality has remained the same.

One can trace Catholic Social Tradition back to Matthew 25. Of course Pope Leo XIII reinforced this with respect to labor. This is an integral part of Augustinian Spirituality. The CST is a memory also. And the memory goes back specifically to the works of mercy (Mt.25). The U.S. bishops have codified this, emphasizing social responsibilities, subsidiarity, life issues, etc. Augustine looks at the human person as made in the image of the triune God. Being so created, a person is made for God; so we are on our way to God and we have life and dignity. The Rule calls us to be a family, and that's important. And there would be a preferential option for the poor.

Augustine's pedagogy

Augustine's love of God is a journey and an experience. We encounter Augustine learning in his journey. It is reflective: there is <u>transformation</u> and <u>diligence</u>. For Augustine this ought to be the nature of learning. Augustine knew the bible. He came to know that God loved him. We can see his education, and perhaps we can imitate him. Living poorly can help.

Augustiniana

We are looking for elements of a common Augustinian spirituality, common that is to the several communities and groups that have a common Augustinian heritage. The Rule is the main binding document. It's an historic document and isn't subject to updating. It gives us focus and direction. The Constitutions extend the Rule to modern day life. They are what distinguish an Augustinian congregation from the others. Aside from orders of men, there are many congregations of women that follow the Rule and their own constitutions. There were no constitutions for the groups Augustine founded. The Fourth Council of the Lateran decreed that no new rule be written. The foundation of the Order was 1244. Leceto and San Leonardo were early foundations. Communities of hermits were spread throughout central Italy. March of that year the Augustinians get a cardinal protector. They don't have these any more. Santa Maria del Popolo was the first OSA foundation in Italy. At the Grand Union of 1256 many groups joined to construct the Order as we know it today. About 356 friars attended. (See The Other Friars by Frances Andrews).

The first Constititutions were written at the General Chapter of Ratisbon in 1290. The spiritual level of this document was very elevated and favorable to a communitarian culture. The word monasterium was never used so as to distinguish the group from monastic foundations. Only clerics were tonsured and could be prior and sub-prior. A very strong emphasis on studies. In 1259 the Order had already acquired a house in Paris close to the university. The same was quickly done re. the other great universities of Europe. By 1284, a decree restricted the number of students. Preachers had to have approval or face some harsh punishments. Augustinians became popular preachers with the underclass particularly in England. Assistants general were gradually adopted mainly as a way to check up on the membership as visitators. This was a time of lay movements and the bishops were getting very concerned over the necessity to supervise preaching and control that.

In the 16th century there was a separatist movement by reform groups. Thus the Recollects got started and the Discalced in Italy. Hugh of St. Victor wrote a commentary on the Rule that became official. To meet new needs of the church some new revisions of the Constitutions were written but now more legalistic and influenced by the Jesuits. After the Vatican Council there was need for revision. This was approved at the chapter of 1968. Fr. Trappe was Prior General at the time. This defined Augustinian charism and the nature of the Order. These constitutions were translated into modern languages and the term Hermits was dropped. There was another revision in 2001. Latin remains the language of the official text.

Chapter 1 of the Constitutions: Origin, nature, charism and witness. We are called to holiness; the aim of the legislation is primarily spiritual. This first part is intended to set the stage and describe the foundation for what follows. So all grows out of a spirituality. All Christians are called to holiness, and there is a specific Augustinian journey. #526 takes up the same theme. Engaging in a fruitful apostolate is part of the road to holiness.

The path we are on is one that we have received. We can say, "that's what is wanted." There is a common spirituality. Authority is to be an exercise of service. All members share in building up the community. So the local house chapter shares in the direction of the community. Part of leadership is to share and draw in the others in leadership. Augustinians are not in the Benedictine tradition. Here with the Augustinians people are called to leadership for a time and then get back into the ranks of the brothers. This is not a hierarchical but a capitular model. And this model has something valuable to teach other institutions and organizations of our world. The foundation for this is the Acts of the Apostles. Augustine continually stressed *humility* for members of the community.

Consecration orients one to community and ministry. We want to bring the Good News to where it needs to go, and we are motivated spiritually. But have we lost some of the importance Augustine gives faith sharing? Certainly Augustine continued to see himself as journeying in faith together with his friends and companions. He wanted lots of sharing and other interactions with his companions. He and Alypius had a great sharing relationship in this respect. Augustine wanted to show people that the call of Jesus and the Acts of the Apostles to community is possible. Thus, emphasis on study and interiority leading to conversion. How available and how flexible are we in terms of the new evangelization? How do we achieve balance in our own lives?

Insignia and habit become visible markers of our unity. They symbolize and enhance our collective spirit.

One can find the Ratio Studiorom on the net or in booklet form. Even though the plan is intended to be universal for the Order, it took a while for this to jell, in fact until after 1989. It was published in 1993 and the General Chapter of 1995 accepted and promulgated the document. All jurisdictions were to bring their formation programs into conformity with the Ratio. In 2007 there was formulated an internet course for formators. Starting now (March 2012) a commission will revisit the document and do some revisioning. The document offers a rich Augustinian heritage and identity. This plan has four sections: an Introduction, common life, the search for God, the vows and the apostolate.

The Introduction: to ensure a common Augustinian identity in formation, and the importance of a common criteria. This facilitates collaboration of jurisdictions. Of course there will be some adjustments each jurisdiction would make based on local culture and other needs. The general objectives get into the spirituality of the Order. The notion of continuing formation is there. But all the formation needs to happen in a community atmosphere. In the Rule there is great respect for the individual and for the group.

Christ and the gospel are to be the center of our lives. Augustine and Augustinian spirituality are means to that end. There needs to be a profound rootedness in Scripture. The community is to be of one mind and one heart intent upon God. Formation to relationships is at the center of community. Examination of prospective candidates takes place prior to admission.

Humility is certainly a necessary ingredient to membership. Otherwise woundedness can get the better of one and growth stops. One area to keep looking at is "individualism." Poverty as a sharing of goods, both material and spiritual is also for some quite a problem. The idea is divestment so as to be better collaborators and people of communion in community. Obedience means sharing in community by looking toward "what is wanted" and showing compassion for one's superiors. Chastity renounces marriage and particularity but is not renouncing affectivity. We're talking here about the search for God in community. It's a pilgrimage, and a good image for this is that of the disciples on journey to Emmaus. Our journey is profoundly personal; that does not translate as private. The Emmaus disciples were for a time in darkness, and then there was illumination when Jesus broke the bread with them. This is an interiority that was shared.

So Augustinians too are called to faith sharing; what's happening to one that might be shared for the enhancement of others. Re. apostolate: one is not what one does. Ministry is a responsibility, a service to the wider community. But the primary service or first work is one's own community; it is a counter balance to the "sociedad de consumo" in which we live. We are looking toward Augustine's *via media* between too much emphasis on the group and too much on the individual. The individual person, nonetheless, must accept primary responsibility for his or her own on-going formation.

And there needs to be an on-going formation accompanied by an on-going conversion as well. It's very Augustinian to put the emphasis on *becoming* rather than *being*. I imagine Augustine too as the first existential phenomenologist. That means that he would tend to always be looking to understand the other and himself based on interiority: how am I being affected by whatever is going on.

Participation in one's own community and circumscription would be the best way to be participating in on-going formation. This greatly helps one avoid burn-out and disillusionment, and also helps prepare one for illness and death.

The Juridical Structure of the Order

The Order of St. Augustine eventually became a clerical order, meaning the majority are clergy rather than brothers. Initially it was not that way; rather the majority were lay people. The Order is still trying to work this out. Structurally, #218 of the Constitutions is clear in that even though the ideal is fraternal equality, some have to hold positions of leadership and so authority. It is not a monastic institute, but is intended to be more part of a society than the monks. So titles like Dom were not acceptable. The habit was to be very simple and practical. And the Order was to be exempt from the bishops for community matters. Its supreme moderator is the prior general as the first among equals. One becomes officially a member of the Order with novitiate, and one is completely a member with solemn profession. Other congregations may be aggregated to the Order by decree of the Father General.

One question to keep in mind: do we as religious bring something special to a local church, or do we tend to simply replicate what the diocesan clergy do? Ideally the community-oriented charism of the Augustinian presence would shine through. Re. kinds of relationships with dioceses, in some places there is tension in other, no.

Presently there are 26 provinces and one abbey. Six of these and the abbey are in suspended government; there are many other jurisdictions, including federations. There are general houses, like Santa Monica, St. Ann's, Cuba, Hippo, Nairobi and some others. The Order's growth and the good of the church are the basic norms determining creation of jurisdictions. Affiliation happens with profession. Ascription happens when one is living in another jurisdiction. The prior general can assign a friar to any house of the Order. There is also government through statutes. The general council with the prior general is the ordinary supervisory authority in the Order. When in session, the general chapter is the highest jurisdictional body.

The Letters of the Priors General and from the many commissions of the Order can be considered official documents of the Order. Looking at the literature of the Order, e.g., the documents of the general councils, one can see a progression of thought regarding the charism of the Order. The General Chapter is the central event in the life of the Order. Unfortunately, more often than not the results of chapters get filed away in community libraries and aren't much read. There's a lot of material available including on Augustinian spirituality. There's now since 1966 an Intermediate General Chapter. This is more exploratory. The Dublin Document (1974) is an important contribution. It has a realistic view of the contemporary world. The Order sees itself as part of the solution rather than as part of the problem. Our mission is to give more testimony to the world about the value of community life. Search for God: a reaction against over materialistic living. Our service includes the joy of believers. Integral love. You can't love God if you don't love your neighbor. Authority is service and bearing others' burdens. We are led to take a critical attitude toward the leadership of the church.

The Chapter of 1989 produced a document on looking toward the new millennium. The Order, as the Church, had been in the process of examining its identity. A central idea was "new frontiers." To boldly face the demands of history with a contemplative spirit, to heed the signs of the times: diminution of vocations, dying of old structures but uncertainty about the future; a moment of discomfort. We don't have to reinvent a foundation but we do need to discover our way into the future. New Augustinians for a new generation. Both the individual and the local community as such must bear witness so as to attract new members. What are the obstacles we need to overcome so as to do this? Is one's ministry too individual or is it done in the name of the community?

13

SIGNS OF THE TIMES

In terms of approach and style, this is a kind of "mixed" chapter: objective *and* personal. The notion that one is to look for the "signs of the times" as a way to discern what God is seeking to accomplish in our world is basically a biblical concept. For example,

> MARK 13.28 "Now of the fig tree learn ye a parable. When the branch thereof is now tender, and the leaves are come forth, you know that summer is very near. 13.29 So you also when you shall see these things come to pass, know ye that it is very nigh, even at the doors."

The intent of this chapter is to briefly describe how the Augustinian Order is attempting to realize its spirituality in our present 21st century and something of the challenges it faces in doing this. A certain summary of Augustinian history and of Augustine's own journey is necessary in order to accomplish this.

Historical Background of the Augustinian Order

The Augustinian way of reflective living was emphasized by the Second Vatican Council and then by a general chapter of the Augustinians. It was certainly a theologically operative premise of St. Augustine in his pastoral work and writings (in particular, The City of God). The world in which Augustine lived was very different from our own in many respects; but in others, quite similar. The province of Africa (now mostly Algeria) was very pluralistic. About half the population were Christian, and half pagan. Of the Christians, about half were Donatist and half were Catholic. Augustine had to deal with all these populations, both as a bishop and one recognized as a civil magistrate accorded the honors given to the governing class. Augustine would have preferred living in a Catholic society, but he didn't.

Several centuries later the Order of Hermits of St. Augustine was officially established (1256). Not much is available of historic record, however, until the General Chapter of Cologne in 1374. From this chapter's written decrees, we do find out that, as far as can be ascertained, for the first time Augustinian friars are encouraged to do "missionary" work, in that the Chapter encourages the members who live close to pagan lands to venture in and preach the gospel to them.

Signs of the Times in Pastoral Ministry

Looking for the "signs of the times" among those dedicated to living an Augustinian spirituality means being dedicated to lifelong learning and critical thinking in the face of historical events. Animating our study is a desire to respond effectively to the concerns of the people of our time. This means we need to be continually in dialogue with them so we can find out about their cares and concerns.

In the General Chapter of 2007, we read: *We need to read together the 'signs of the times'* that offer on one hand, opportunities, and, on the other hand, challenges for the mission of the Church."* Ordinary General Chapter 2007, 1.3

There are some general "signs of the times," shared by all people, and more importantly in terms of particular pastoral planning and response to needs and signs particular to each culture. For example, I've been at a parish in Los Angeles for a number of years. I think I am observing a couple of related trends: some parishioners who are looking for exactness religiously and theologically and who are not comfortable with much ambiguity and whose tendency is toward literalism; and some parishioners who want nuance, participation in setting goals, theological speculation and a concerted move toward more inclusion of the feminine, collaborative decision-making and ministry. The first group is more comfortable with a paternalistic leadership style, the second is not; the pastoral challenge, it seems to me, is to hold on to both, gearing pastoral approaches to each one. For instance, by being more inviting to inclusion in parish ministry of the first group might help them move away from literalism; by providing somewhat challenging adult education offerings for the second group and parish committees and councils that are open to dialogue and consensus. Probably the most challenging area for the clergy in this parish is the Sunday homily, because the congregation is going to be looking and hoping for so much: acceptance of all segments of the population (single, married, gay, straight, old, young, white, black, Latino, Filipino, Italian, Armenian, Oriental, etc.), a good grasp of doctrine, how to contextualize the readings historically, showing concern and compassion, not being paternalistic, being inviting and welcoming, respectful of American values but not being nationalistic, open to new members especially immigrants, keeping attention, etc.

Over the years much of the more affluent white population has moved elsewhere. The parish school is now mostly Filipino and Latino with some children from white or mixed families and some Armenian children. But from a high of 300 or so students a few years ago, the school population is now down to 123 students, including kindergarten.

There is a sizable population of homeless and economically deprived people in the area or gravitating in and out. We are fortunate in that the St. Vincent de Paul organization is very well organized and ready to respond to this population.

Ecumenically the parish has good relations with the local Lutheran congregation whose church building is also a venue for the American Catholic Church, with the Sikhs whose temple is just a block away, and with the Anglicans who are in the process of being welcomed into the Anglo Catholic Ordinariate of the U.S. The parish has been open for many years to the active participation of Armenian rite Catholics and their Armenian Apostolic neighbors and relatives, and both groups feel welcome to full participation. Once a year an Armenian rite Liturgy of the Eucharist is celebrated on the feast of St. Rita of Cassia for whom the Armenians have special devotion. We have Greek Catholic, Maronite, and sometimes members of other rites as well. There's a Ukrainian Catholic church, a Russian Orthodox, Armenian Apostolic and a Coptic church not far away. Los Angeles, like Augustine's Africa and specifically Hippo, is also very pluralistic. On any given Sunday Mass is celebrated in the archdiocese in 61 different languages.

Reenchanting the Universe

One prolific contemporary thinker and author whom I've heard speak a number of times at the Assisi Seminars, Irvin Laszlo, is particularly concerned about the over-emphasis in contemporary culture of the purely rational and materialistic. I list some of his works in the Suggested Reading section of this paper. For purposes here I want to refer to his <u>Science and the Reenchantment of the Cosmos: The Rise of the Integral Vision of Reality</u>. In his Introduction Laszlo writes:

> "At the cutting edge of contemporary science a remarkable insight is surfacing: the universe, with all things in it, is a quasi-living, coherent whole. All things in it are connected. All that happens in one place also happens in other places; all that happened at one time happens at all other times. And the traces of all things that ever happened endure; nothing is entirely evanescent, here today and vanished tomorrow."
> (Laszlo, Ervin, <u>Science and the Reenchantment of the Cosmos: The Rise of the Integral Vision of Reality</u> (p. 2). Inner Traditions Bear & Company. Kindle Edition).

This quote from Laszlo presents the notion of Quantum very succinctly. I had some inkling of what he's describing before I heard him speak or read any of his work. But reading him I can understand that his grasp of this is very broad and scientific. It's clear too that he's not just pushing a theory but rather reacting to what he perceives as most dehumanizing, the ignoring of the spiritual dimension, the claim that what you can see and measure is real, what you can't is not real. I want to add one further sentence:

"In ages past the connectedness and wholeness of the world was known to medicine men, priests, and shamans, to seers and sages, and to all people who had the courage to look beyond their nose and stay open to what they saw."

Aristotle goes to Paris

I think if one can rise above history somewhat and take in the "big picture," one could imagine what Laszlo is saying. Tribal peoples never lost a sense of enchantment, but those peoples affected by the scientism and materialism of Western culture did. I can imagine looking at historical events up to the re-discovery of Aristotle in the Middle Ages in Baghdad, imagine traders and scholars taking the texts in Arabic translation to Spain, seeing them translated into Latin by scholars there, and then making their way to the University of Paris where Albert and Thomas Aquinas studied them and came under their spell.

In the centuries that followed, with new discoveries in astronomy and other sciences (Galileo, Bacon), and in philosophy, economics and political theory (Descartes, Marx), and in the natural sciences (Darwin), in a trajectory begun by Aristotle and some translators in Bagdad, the Western world became "disenchanted." Note well that Augustine and his spirituality and Jung and his theorizing do not buy into this kind of a world. They are rather the principal anchors linking us to Platonic thought, the oldest theorizing around the idea of an interconnected and enchanted cosmos in Western thought (though not as old as the oldest Hindu scriptures which go back several thousand years before the Christian era). Many advances in science and medicine and new inventiveness can be traced to Aristotelian thinking and the discipline that goes with it. So this is not meant to dismiss all that tradition. But it is to mourn a great loss, and to want to reconnect with a way of being and envisioning that is more in conformity with the way things really are. And the presence of the creative grace of God in Christ permeates all that is as well.

Some Contemporary Social Critics

There are certain trends in contemporary sociological and philosophical critical thinking, particularly European, that again remind me of the Augustinian via media, between Donatism and Pelagius. Three of these thinkers are Zygmunt Bauman, Jurgen Habermas and Slavoj Zizek, the first two German, the last Slovenian. Though differing from each other in emphasis and details, what they have in common is a desire to make some accommodation between secular society and religion, to help contribute to a respectful dialogue. This imperative is coming out of their reflections on modernity, on the failure of the Enlightenment and of the scientism and rationalism that went along with it, to produce a truly happier brave new world and improve qualitatively the human social condition. Part of their critique, a substantial part, concludes that we need to return to or at least reestablish some sort of a way whereby religions can contribute to society in a substantial way. The Pope would respond positively to this kind of initiative as he too sees the need for such an ongoing dialogue, believing that both parties, religion and civil society, need each others' insights and contributions for the sake of health, equilibrium and growth.

These thinkers, and I imagine the Pope would agree, are convinced that the "disenchantment" of modernity that has come about through the Enlightenment and the pure rationality that has accompanied it, have paved the way for modern horrors such as the Holocaust, the excesses of Capitalism and environmental catastrophes. Recall that an out of balance rationality that downplays the importance of the feeling function and of soul and intuitive responses and instincts make the human being into an automaton, a machine; that it is feeling balanced with reason that truly humanizes.

It seems to me that underneath it all, as a holistic or quantum response, that the solution would be a return to Augustine's spirituality, especially with its emphasis on seeking a *via media* between humanism (read Pelagius) and fundamentalism (read Donatism), and an admission that ultimately we need to grant the sovereignty and ultimacy of God alone and the workings of grace. And, of course, also of the essence of any Augustinian spirituality is a fundamental option for the most oppressed and marginated, for the outcast and the stranger among us. This approach to spirituality might well be attractive to non-Christians as well.

Augustine did not write out his sermons. He had stenographers present in the basilica taking notes on wax tablets, and he would later redact them. Most of the dockworkers that attended Augustine's basilica were illiterate. He wouldn't get into very difficult topics in his sermons but reserved them for his writings. And he wrote his books for the most part because requested to do so by one of his friends. So his sermons were not theological arguments. They were intended to be persuasive toward leading a moral life. And in terms of instructing, his advice was to get more vociferous as the topic became more crucial. To keep attention one has to switch emphasis and tone. Reading Augustine one can miss these emphases; the books were first met to be read aloud, not privately, so innuendos can be missed easily. Delivery is meant to unite speaker and hearer: each of us comes to dwell in the other.

Prayer is an important part of delivery for Augustine; the speaker must pray for himself and for the hearers. The deliverer is also a hearer, and he seeks to find out how the hearers are hearing. De Catechisandis Rudibus is the best source for this, written at the request of a friend, Deo Gratias. This book is about educating people interested in the faith or preparing for baptism. So it's a mixed audience of illiterate people and more or

126

less educated. There was no formal RCIA in those days; rather the sermon was everything. So Augustine gives some advice about method and then some examples. Deo Gratias asked for this and got it. 1 Cor. 9:7 God loves a cheerful giver, Augustine uses as part of a needed method for successful delivery of a message meant to catechize. When one is preaching one is bringing the mercy of God to others.

Augustine tends to be eschatological, so he aims us at the "rest." People need courage to confront the difficulties of life. We are called to delight in the Good News that God loves us. We can catch fire thus for love of God knowing that God has loved us first. When in the state of equality with God, he emptied himself, becoming weak so as to gain the weak. "To everyone a mother," Augustine compares the speaker, tailoring style to many different groups of hearers. So the speaker seeks to be calm toward those who need to be taught and un-taught. (Augustine is called the hammer of error (later, heretics). Simple teaching, polemics and apologetics; these people need the calm of reason (unlike contemporary U.S. political discourse). Moderate style: use ornate language, poetics, etc. not to win over the hostile but to attract the recalcitrant. Anagogy and allegory work here. Anagogy means to lead and to lift up. All is summed up in "You shall love your neighbor as yourself." The grand style, how are you going to live the faith; to do something about it. Here you take the already convinced and persuade them to have one mind and heart; for people who need and can take a tough message. To implore, rebuke and encourage.

1 Cor. 12: 1-10. That there are different gifts, different services, etc. To each person, particularized gifts for the good of the community. And all from one and the same Spirit. One of the principal charisms of the Augustinian tradition is *prophecy*, meaning an ability and inclination to interpret the *signs of the times*. In pastoral ministry one is required to discern more particularly one's own charisms, and to seek ministry that corresponds to that. If one finds oneself in some ministry that just doesn't seem to fit, then some discernment is certainly in order. And sometimes one is just going to have to seek out a ministry that is a good fit. And if no such ministry is available or even existing, then maybe some creativity is in order, so one looks elsewhere beyond the traditional group or community or religious jurisdiction. Nonetheless, wherever one works and in whatever ministry, community living is providing the energy for living in the Spirit.

Augustinian Pastoral Theology

Theology is faith seeking understanding, according to St. Anselm. In the Letter to the Hebrews we also have a reflective definition. Faith brings us beyond the senses; to trust in those things unheard and unseen: the substance of things hoped for. According to Karl Rahner: explanation and explication of what has been received. This also means "unfolding." We are in a relationship with God such that we are partners with God, with mind and heart both in relationship. There's biblical theology, spirituality, moral theology, systematic theology, historical theology and pastoral theology. From the pastoral point of view, the intellectual must be blended with a spirituality of the heart. Pastoral ministers particularly are called to do this.

There are many specific pastoral tasks that flow from a theology of pastoral theology, and one can organize these in broad categories or just list specific tasks in a kind of practical way. Another way of looking at this is to focus generally on how one is or can be with others in a pastoral way. So a minister could be with others without being focused on a task, maybe just encouraging, or trying to listen or figure out areas of needs and interests. Some people speak of the practice or *praxis* of ministry. However, ministry is not only practice, it is also *being*. Introduction to the Practice of Ministry is a good resource for this. Also, one can organize tasks into *knowing, doing and being*. These can be termed charisms, meaning *gifts*. Some tasks rely on one charism and not so much on the others. The seven gifts of the Holy Spirit can also be a good way to organize ministry tasks.

Teaching: One should know one's subject; one should be able to communicate with the particular group with whom one is working; one needs the gift of *humility*; and one can see how archetypes are at work here: ego, Self, the Wise person, the Teacher, the Creator, persona, and many more; and the less there is of you, the more there can be of God. Augustine is very big on *humility*. He sees this as preceding, accompanying and following up on all we do. And *humility* means not hiding behind things in order to terrorize people or just distance them; it means not taking up too much psychological space.

Preaching: One needs to know the scriptures, and the particular group for whom one is preaching, the signs of the times, contemporary events, the people's struggles, joys and hopes. One should include some stories: one's own, the people's, and God's story. Also there needs to be truth-telling. If the preacher does not believe what is being preached, the people can discern this. In Sermon 339 Augustine speaks of preaching and accuracy. It's nice to be affirmed, but Augustine warns against putting too much importance on being complimented. Is preaching a ministry? It is a very important one, and from the active parishioner's point of view, just about the most important thing for them during a week.

Care: forgiveness, healing and joy are a real part of our world. How do we work at reconciliation in our world? Often people seeking some kind of assistance at a church are broken through no fault of their own. We are called to compassion, not to cynicism or doubt. Part of human nature is that one wants to be comfortable. Often being with the suffering disrupts one's comfort. Using body analogy, when one part hurts, the other parts are affected. And any group or organization or society is the same. If one part is damaged, all the rest is affected.

Prayer & Worship: It's important in liturgical communities to abide by the rubrics and other traditions, and to not deviate too much because this is not the private prayer of the minister but the public prayer of the church. Being present to and with the movement of the liturgy is of great importance. Adoration is the *being* part of worship. Ideally, this will be filled with reverence and awesomeness. This will hopefully be the case during Eucharist. Cfr. Sermon 272, where Augustine speaks of the people as the body of Christ.

Social: Mercy & Justice: This has to do with global solidarity and the role of civil society to watch out for the care of the people. The churches want to collaborate in this. Much of this is advocacy; one is called to use tactics for the sake of justice. Seeing Jesus in others is the *being* part.

Deus Caritas Est was Pope Benedict's first encyclical, and it is very Augustinian.

Administration. Though necessary, these tasks can distract easily and greatly from the mission of some ministry; and not all have the talent of administration. One must have the vision of how things *can* be, not just *are*. In Augustine's thought, one's particular exercise of ministry must have some connection with one's community. Those in the exercise of authority are to think of themselves as in a service for the rest. (Cfr. Kathleen Cahalan Introducing the Practice of Ministry)

Augustine's Conversion

Augustine had grown disillusioned with his life as rhetor, and he went out to a country estate called Cassaga Brianza (Cassiciacum). This is probably 386. If he was baptized in April of 387, then there's about a year of dialogs from this time. These are conversations on themes like happiness. Re. pastoral ministry, what is it that brings us happiness? We know it is Nov. 13, 354 that he was born because here in De Beata Vita he writes that his friends took him to his birthday party. This was for Augustine a restful period and a long retreat. He decided during this time to request baptism. During the baptism the *Te Deum* was sung.

One can best understand Augustine in light of his conversion. His spirituality developed out of this impetus. Augustine matters because his spirituality matches his practice, or, better, his practice matches his spirituality. There is a unity, an integrity about him. To a great extent in his Confessions, Augustine is doing an *exercitatio mentis,* a mind experiment. He did this even publicly, while preaching and in conversation with friends. In some ways he was doing theological exploration. He was unique among Christian thinkers in beginning his reflections with his birth rather than his baptism. He saw God working in him and in his experiences all through his life leading up to his baptism. His life, preaching and doctrine had to include others since his conversion did.

Augustine puts a lot of emphasis on *desire*. And to be conscious of waiting on God. He was getting at the importance of stretching one's mind and heart. Waiting and desire can exercise the mind and heart. And figuring out what's involved in waiting and desiring helps bring one to greater consciousness. So, why does Augustine matter? I think we can easily see ourselves in him. He says things in his Confessions that we have all wanted to say, he speaks of thoughts and feelings we have all felt and thought, but maybe concluded we shouldn't talk about. He speaks of "delight." As the emperor's spokesperson he was supposed to delight his audience. Whether as a preacher he continued to want to delight, probably not in the same way. More than delight, he wanted to be complete and accurate and exhort the people to right thinking and right living.

Getting back to desires: which do you pay attention to and which do you try to avoid? Desires which are not healthy tend to be destructive. But a good question to ask of desire: do we have the means to get to the object of our desire? Does the object of our desire have a permanence? Augustine used the analogy of Jesus' cross as a "craft" in which we can cross the eternal sea and come to God.

"Daily bread" for Augustine meant our daily human needs for sustenance, whether physical or spiritual. The Eucharist is daily bread. And when really our daily bread, we will become what we eat. All of life is in some way sacramental. Hymns, Eucharist and scripture are all our daily bread.

Sermon 21. To desire God must include a desire for those who are of God. Augustine, as most preachers, finds his words are influenced also by the people who are present. And even the preacher must be nourished by what is said. At times the preacher may even be surprised at what he or she says. And, though mostly silent, there is interaction in and among the hearers. Augustine suggests that the people listen to him more as a fellow learner than as a master (teacher). He suggests they are engaged in a common work. He says that even though a mother delights in nursing her child, she doesn't want it to remain forever an infant. He says that to begin to treat God as a friend, one will be less inclined to think of God as a puppeteer. So welcome God into your house. And God will give you even more room by coming. You'd think God would be so large as to crowd one out, yet the opposite is true. And Christ speaks through the preacher. We hear him with the ears of the heart. And since we are all Christ, when one speaks or sings, it is somehow Christ who is speaking through one. "But I don't want to be saved without you." He is asking for some sort of solidarity with the people; as he is intent in stirring up salvation in the hearers, so he wants them to try to do the same thing. He asks them to not make light of their sins. Even if no one else sees these things, God sees them.

Augustine and the Eucharist

For Augustine Eucharist is implicit everywhere; he does not specifically focus on this as though a separate phenomenon from the rest of life. He speaks of Eucharist in preparing catechumens and in City of God Book 10 when comparing Christian to pagan sacrifice. Also in the early Church Eucharist was not to be talked about except with those already initiated as Christians. So one might preach on some aspect of Eucharist, or instruct newly baptized, but one would not respond to questions about it coming from non-Christians, nor write on it if one's writings would likely become available publicly. In some cities of the Empire by the time of Bishop Augustine Mass would be celebrated daily. Augustine insinuated that Monica went to church daily. When Augustine speaks about assisting the poor and marginated, he is implicitly speaking of the Eucharist. If one could read his mind and heart, Augustine's experience is of Eucharist everywhere. And Augustine pays more attention to those present for Eucharist than what happens on the altar. He is concerned more about their transformation into the Body of Christ than he is about what happens to the bread and wine on the altar. Even as a catechumen Augustine had a sophisticated sense of Eucharist, that what we receive doesn't become part of us, rather we become what we receive.

Augustine has lots to say about Eucharist. He doesn't deny the validity of Donatist Eucharist, but he did feel they had something lacking due to poor leadership and a certain pride. Not that Catholic Christians don't suffer from this at times too. For Augustine Eucharist eaten among the poor is a way of saying "I need God." And one has this need in particular due to sinfulness. The Donatists felt they couldn't or ought not admit their sinfulness. Augustine had no problem admitting his. "You are baked into the bread which is the body of Christ." His focus is on the receivers, on the community and their and his experience of what is going on. So Augustine is most concerned with the transformation going on in the people, in their interiority. Probably in the back of Augustine's mind is "hospitality." He sees this as something reciprocal. Each has something which comes from the exchange. It's like hungering and thirsting for justice. I don't give because I'm better and you don't receive because you're inferior. Maybe we too can think this way of Eucharist, in terms of hospitality.

"The faithful know the body of Christ if they are acting as the body of Christ," Augustine says in a homily on John's gospel. Much of his commentary is in the context of concern about how Catholics and Donatists are treating each other. One can bridge this to our own contemporary relationships with other Christians. Almost always Augustine is concerned with experience rather than theory. I think there's something important in this for contemporary believers. I mean the sharing of experiences will usually come across better than theory. And the example of Augustine as someone who lived and breathed scripture and Eucharist is for us today quite a good example, lest one's religion become too much a thing of the head rather than the whole person. So Quantum-wise, holistically, we are called to be people of faith in head and heart, in faith and works, and in the context of community. The Eucharist reminds us of this. And the Eucharist reminds us of *friendship*.

This gets us back again to the question of "interiority." Augustine's sense of this was very social and community oriented. Moments and times of silence can help interiority, provided it's used for reflection and contemplation. Many, maybe most people find moments of silence in a community gathering as uncomfortable. Yet everyone needs times of silence. It's like silence creates space, inner space, leading to more authenticity and integrity.

St. Teresa of Avila was educated by the Augustinian nuns of Avila. There she read and studied the Confessions. She said she saw herself in them. Particularly she saw herself in him at the point he recounts his conversion experience. That's what Augustine wanted, that the readers would see themselves in his experiences. There are a multitude of translations, each one offering different insights. Some are quite difficult to read, esp. those at the turn of 19th-20th centuries. For some Augustine's Neo-Platonic philosophy is difficult or his self-castigation may be off-putting.

The Confessions are best read slowly and contemplatively. It was written many centuries ago, yet it's still modern. People never tire of reading this book because it is always contemporary. The entire book is written as a long prayer; he addresses God mostly and occasionally the reader. It seems to be God the Father whom he is addressing. "You have made us for yourself and our hearts are restless until they rest in you." He is not so much confessing his sins as he is praying for and thanking God for mercy and grace. He speaks of his desires, and his resistance, and finally his acceptance of grace. "You knew what I was suffering, and no one else knew it." The book is written for us. In book 10, he writes how his words might stir up one's heart, make people aware of their weakness, and conscious of forgiveness. This is about how grace transforms real people. He recounts how reading of or hearing other peoples' accounts of their conversions also moved him. The Confessions are immersed in scripture, inextricably at times.

In his writing he wears different hats: as pilgrim, as bishop, as common man, as a monk. So different passages reflect different aspects of the man. Guardini says we must recognize both Augustine's sensuality and his predisposition to religion in order to understand him. Behind the known Augustine senses the unknown. Much of his society was pagan. He wasn't baptized and his knowledge of the faith was from his mother. Intellectual conversion and moral conversion were both part of his being. Now, how do we today connect with others as Augustine did on the basis of his deepest thinking and values?

Augustine reflecting on his inborn talents and desires makes one reflect on one's own inborn traits, not to become proud but to simply be aware and give thanks for whatever they are. He says he hated to be wrong. Yet he also admits being very judgmental of others who make mistakes.

The last three books of the Confessions seem unrelated to the previous books. Book 13 is a kind of recapitulation of what went before. It's very Holy Spirit centered. He's looking to make sure the meaning of baptism is clear and not dependent on the minister (Donatism). Baptism is situated in God, not in particularities of ministers or places. Augustine described his own baptism in book 9. His description is very brief. And he is writing in a predominately Donatist city. In book 13 he is reading Genesis through the eyes of Paul. He's saying, "this is what happened to me in baptism," and he is celebrating baptism in general as God's continual work on creation, in this case God's work drawing and purifying people, and drawing them into the kingdom.

It's likely c. 397 as Augustine is writing his Confessions. The Donatists are casting aspersions on Augustine as though he were still a Manichaean. So Augustine stresses the goodness of creation, a stand directly opposite that of the Manichaeans. This stress of his was a way, in fact, of saying that he was *not* a *Manichaean*.

In Sermon 68 Augustine describes Jesus confessing to the Father. He wasn't confessing sins, but who he was and a confession of praise. We can do the same thing: confess our sins, but also our praising and other aspects of human experience. The "confessional" as a location in space is just a few centuries old, and maybe gives us a rather limited sense of *confession*.

Sermon 23a: let us do what we pray and sing. Let us not go to church if it doesn't make any difference. Isn't confessing to God being honest with God and with oneself, saying in effect this is the way I am, or this is how I've acted? God loves the sinner, but not the sin.

In Sermon 389: here Augustine is encouraging people to be unified in mind and heart around the Word, such that it becomes completely part of one, so that there's a memory of the words of scripture and an adherence of love and affection for the words. In all likelihood the sermon was given shortly after the sack of Rome so there would have been many refugees there in Hippo listening to him. He doesn't use the word Eucharist in the homily, but he clearly has this in the back of his mind. The nourishment he's speaking of is God's grace, always available, always ready to nourish. He's suggesting that the hearers are lacking in prayer; maybe that they are thinking of prayer as specific prayers they recite, and he is thinking of prayer in much broader terms, including in assisting the poor.

Augustine is also vividly suggesting in this homily the basic equality of all people, and the need to give out of this equality and not to consider oneself as somehow superior because one gives and another receives. And there is the aspect of generosity, so one receives if one gives. And when you give to the poor you will have advocacy in heaven. So Augustine is trying to shake some of his hearers loose from thinking that they are somehow morally superior because they are helping others. The sack of Rome was in the year 410. Gift to the poor: is this not Eucharist? I think from Augustine's point of view all generosity and loving action is doing Eucharist. So this is kind of a commentary on Matthew's gospel of judgment: I was hungry, I was thirsty, I was naked, etc.

"Unless you believe you shall not understand." Or... "Endure." Augustine is encouraging the hearers to walk by faith so they may reach the truth that endures. There are different kinds of faith. Starting after the great persecution Christians started having a need to resolve the great Christological questions and then the great Trinitarian questions, esp. of the Spirit. Preachers and teachers tried to explain these things and they needed to treat ordinary Christians as capable of understanding these things. There was preaching, teaching and exile, and exile too became a form of teaching. If terminology was not received, it did not teach. Each generation repeats this phenomenon of preaching and teaching so that the faith is transmitted again and again. People do start off having already some kind of curiosity motivated by faith. Without rudimentary faith there can be no action, no movement. Much of sermon 43 is about belief. He speaks of difference between heresy and belief, holding the truth, a burning passion of Augustine since his youth.

He wants to demonstrate that the Manichaeans are acting irrationally when they attack the Catholic faith. He is in the sermon trying to deal with people whose faith is changing, maturing. Something we have to deal with quite a bit today. How does one speak of the value of faith? Is there anything more important than the gift of faith? Maybe life itself. I like to use here the analogy or metaphor of glasses. Faith is like glasses. You put them on and you see better. Or let Christ be the judge of these things; listen to him. A typical Augustinian process is to go to God's word rather than rely on reason. When Augustine gave up on the Manichees, he went to the philosophers (Neo-Platonism), and then he returned to scripture and to Christ. Then he can talk about faith seeking understanding.

People come to worship to express their faith but they don't always realize how fragile their faith is. It needs to be strengthened. "Help my unbelief." Cleverly Augustine plays with words. But the ending and even the beginning seem truncated, as though we don't have the whole sermon. We the teachers are not too different from the people we teach. It's a good practice to reflect on others' and one's own faith journey, and thus one can be both a better teacher and a better learner.

Summary of Chapter

I see the main relevance for living an Augustinian spirituality today whether as a professed religious or as a lay person, aside from personal call and individual growth in faith, as participating in an ever new paradigm that does tend, little by little, to push aside less desirable paradigms such as that of patriarchy. And the great mass of Augustine's writings, of so many of his followers and the history of the Augustinian movement and Order, all point in the direction of encouraging people to live concretely the Christian life espoused in the Acts of the Apostles.

14

ON A MORE PERSONAL NOTE

It is in the nature of a study such as this that the author keep a handle on objectivity and avoid getting too personal. I think I've maintained that separation fairly well, even to the extent of not being too revelatory about the dream material I've presented. But now, as I am getting some closure on this work, I would like to dedicate a few pages to the more personal. My idea is to look for dream material and synchronicities from my own experience and as inspired by Assisi events, my course work and experiences connected with the Institute of Augustinian Spirituality, and from my reading, and then write them up here. I also will describe some instances in which I am seeking to apply quantum and depth psychological principles to myself.

As I write some of the following section, I'm in Brattleboro, Vermont, at an Assisi Conference on the New Sciences. Today we heard from Dr. Richard Ott, and tomorrow, Dr. F. David Peat will be sharing his thoughts with us. Today's presentation was really great. I met F. David this evening at a wine & cheese party.

As I listen to the presenters, I am also wondering how this paper I'm writing might manifest some of the qualities they're talking about, especially those qualities centrally held dear by the Assisi community. For example, would my study help further redemption work in some way? I think it would, in so far as it might serve as a guide and introduction to depth psychological thought and spirituality for students, educational staffs and faculties and other interested readers. From the outset, my intent has been to produce something of a handbook for that purpose, and I think it is for the most part clear and self-explanatory.

When I've written previous papers, theses and a dissertation, I never went back and re-read them once they were completed and submitted. Nor did I particularly enjoy composing them. By contrast, this paper I've reviewed numerous times and I must admit I've enjoyed the writing and I consider the content very important and crucial for human and other planetary life. So I'd say that some rather positive and deeply spiritual fields get constellated for me as I reflect on this material.

Quantum thought describes reality as circular, or, better yet, as spiral. So does depth psychology. And I would regard this work in that same light: there are some central themes around which my observations circumambulate as I develop them. It contains a weaving of conceptual iterations that eventually culminate in some "conclusions" derived from Quantum Theology, Depth Psychology and Augustinian Spirituality.

I have had a general plan in putting this opus together, but I've also tried to be open (which for me is not easy), to the idea that "life" might well have some intentions for me in this regard; or, considering this work as an objectively existent entity, I've had to enquire: what is wanted, what is being called for in a work like this, what is pushing to get expressed, and not so much what do *I* want to say.

The presenters have been speaking of the forces of electricity and magnetism and their inter-relationship to each other and to light. So by way of this Quantum analogy, I wonder if and to what extent this paper will shed any light in some significant way for those who read it? Some people have told that it's quite clear and readable and that they have appreciated reading it. I hope that continues to be true. F. David mentioned that the artist Cezanne considered himself in his work to be the consciousness of nature. I think good writing on life-significant material is also a making-conscious, to a large extent, of that which lies, to a more or less degree, under the surface of things.

F. David Peat also mentioned "projective identification," that phenomenon (usually spoken of in relation to psychotherapy), whereby one person feels like another has gained entrance to his or her psyche and is experienced as somehow within or as leaving some "content" within. I have this experience with some frequency, and not just in counseling situations, and others have told me the same with respect to feeling something of me within them. By way of analogy, I hope the several personages I've mentioned and described in these pages "come alive" somehow for the reader because it is that experience that, among others, helps people get distance from both alienation and narcissism. The speaker was pondering about what might be the relationship of field theory to this experience of projective identification. I would think that if such an experience is of a positive nature, that there is present a kind of love field. Of course, one might also feel "caught" in another's space or even "possessed" by some projection. Whatever those fields might be, they sometimes feel dark and negative.

I especially enjoyed Peat's thoughts on Pauli, on Pauli's interest in symmetry and the experiments into the sub-atomic entities of bozons and fermions, and how the bozons are positive seekers and joiners and the fermions, negative distancers and rather "unfriendly." And I mentioned that a clear correspondence to that phenomenon is found in Taoism in the yin/yang apparent duality system. David referred to the bozon/fermion reality as the underlying material archetype. I think he's right, and, again, one might say that even *that* concept fits within the Taoist insight regarding all reality. And this archetypal force is certainly present at the human level as well, as everyone oscillates between attractions and repulsions, joining and separating. I don't know what one might do with neutrinos by way of metaphor, since neutrinos have neither a positive nor a negative charge: they are between yin and yang, kind of like a new synthesis that refuses to yield to a new thesis-antithesis. Well, I suppose once in a while I've felt a bit neutrino-like, but it doesn't seem to last.

I was recently observing an exchange in which someone was really getting into another's "face." Our "Self" is sensitive, like sub-atomic entities: look too closely or without the right attitude, and the Self just disappears and is no longer available. On the other hand I have experienced interventions "in my face" but clearly by someone who cared, and the Self, in effect, came out of alienation/hiding and rather revealed its more authentic nature. So, it seems, analogically, the Self and other archetypes and their complexes sometimes react like fermions and sometimes like bozons.

I have alluded to the phenomenon of synchronicity in these pages (see Chap. 3), and now I'd like to describe that from a more personal angle. If you recall, synchronicity refers to those attention-getting, strange, inexplicable experiences wherein one or more seemingly unrelated events (thus no apparent causality), occur together. One such event you might hear about with some frequency is that of someone's beloved clock stopping at exactly the person's moment of death. My example is not as dramatic. It went like this: For quite a long period of time while in college seminary I couldn't seem to shake off a rather persistent depression ("nigredo" in alchemy). Then one bright, cool spring day an older faculty member, kind of a mentor of mine, invited me to go with him to the university gym for a swim. I'd done this with him many times. He loved playing catch while treading water and, in fact, he had the ability to float like a cork.

So we went. I was ready before him so I went into the large pool area. It's impossible to convey in words what my experience was, except to give a description as best I can. Sunlight was streaming in through some glass panels in the roof, the smell of chlorine was oddly pleasant for a change, and the water as I dove in, was just a perfect temperature for a cool day, probably around 85 degrees. Talk about a baptism! My sensation was one of complete peace and union with the water, the air, the sunlight, the chemicals, everything, and a kind of intuition that my depression was gone, that I had passed through some trial and come out on the other side.

Now, was this an experience of synchronicity? I think it was, although how to name it is not the important thing. But something did happen to me that I experienced as deeply transforming and there is no necessary causal connection between what happened experientially and swimming pool, sunlight, water and temperature. I'm very grateful for the experience, and for me it was redemptive and freeing, and, in hindsight I can see how it does fit into a phase of the alchemical tradition. It would certainly be wonderful to have more of those experiences, but they can't be planned or manufactured; they are pure gift.

I imagine that another way of looking at the phenomenon I am describing is to see it as an intervention by what Jung terms the "transcendent function," and by what Christian theology names as the Holy Spirit, and that the context is that of moving, by way of a healing, from the effects of alienation to that of emotional/psychic and spiritual salvation. The only attitude that makes sense to me in light of such an experience is that of gratitude. I am also reminded of an idea, which is that the best things in life just happen, they can't be produced at will: love is a by-product, as are other closely connected deep experiences like "community." They happen when other things are present, like commitment and a willingness to sacrifice. You can set up some conditions and hope for the best, but redemptive experiences come as grace.

I think both Augustine and Jung would be in agreement on the above. But Jung is not mostly interested in theology or metaphysics. He takes religious doctrines and dogmas and looks at them metaphorically for their psychological implications. Thus Jung's and the Jungians' fascination with the Christian Trinity or with the Assumption of Mary are best understood as pointing to inner movements of the human psyche, and in the case of the Assumption, in particular with the vital importance of the feminine in divine and human life (now that a human woman (the feminine) is forever with God.

I am also feeling influenced by St. Augustine in this chapter as I write some personal thoughts. Especially I feel influenced by his Confessions. In large measure Augustine wrote very personally about himself, his sins and failures, and his experience of the divine, in order to influence others in their search for God. I have something like that in mind too. I would like to influence people to look at themselves introspectively in the light of the psychological, social and physical sciences so as to better prepare a foundation for theological investigations and education. I am thinking here in particular of people in formation programs of various kinds, such as seminaries, deacon formation and lay leadership training programs. I think probably Augustine didn't intellectually separate out the psychological from the spiritual aspects of his spirituality. But in so far as possible, I think it's a good idea to help provide people with good human formation prior to their entering into theological education lest they get caught up into an overly spiritualized paradigm and forget their humanity and status as cultural and embodied beings.

A question I have and the answer to which I don't, is: how is the experience of synchronicity a doorway to the unconscious? Well, maybe I do have an answer at least in part and using the example I just gave: synchronicities indicate movement within one's objective unconscious; they indicate (or, at least may indicate), a rearrangement of inner entities (e.g., ego, self and transcendent function in relationship), such that a balance is either restored or a new more healthy synthesis produced. Synchronicities, if they are genuine, are not manufactured by people, but rather have their own objectivity and are to be looked at and translated for their meaning that way. I think art in all its forms is of the same nature. What I mean is that once produced, unless it is purely egoic, a work of art is there to be seen and appreciated for itself, quite apart from whoever might have produced it. Knowing something about the artist might well help in grasping hidden, more unconscious meanings of the piece, but it still stands on its own in an objective sense.

I recently wrote a short poem and felt in the process that it was more writing itself. Looking at what I wrote subsequently, I was startled though also excited by what it was telling me about myself. The short poem was serving as a mirror to my unconscious in a not too flattering way, but the opportunities for self-knowledge were clear after some discussion about it. The poem was pointing to some "puer" issues that need to be paid attention to. So, as with other art forms, poetry, like dreams and synchronicity, is a doorway to the unconscious.

One archetypal field I have felt enveloped in during the past several years is that of "thanatos", or death. My sister, brother and then mother all died within a four-year period. Then the sale of the housing project where I had worked for four years started impacting me as well by way of the death field. Apparently I wasn't dealing with this very well on a conscious level, and quite suddenly and unexpectedly one evening during Mass for All Souls Day (Dia de los muertos), at Villa Nueva housing project, I pretty much came unglued during my homily (sermon). I don't feel comfortable being weepy even with close friends, and I was terribly embarrassed to find I couldn't control my tears in a public setting. The culture there, however, is quite accepting of public emotional displays. It must have been overall, however, a salutary experience, because within a short time that evening I was feeling very relieved and happy. It was as though this emotive, mourning experience had freed me from the death field. I am really grateful for that, even though I am still reluctant to be so expressive publicly of my emotions.

That kind of experience, not intended and beyond ego manufacture and control, also gives one a glimpse into the world of the unconscious, the non-manifest. And like the other realities of dreams, synchronicities, and art, it can serve as a doorway and a heightener of consciousness.

I'd like to point out that Mexican culture celebrates The Day of the Dead in a very unique way, usually (and all the following were present) with an altar or table on which photos of the deceased are placed, little skulls and skeletons made of sugar, and often more and more, some Halloween symbols indicating U.S. influence. What I want to convey is that there was quite a field created in many ways, including by way of symbols, and people remembering their deceased relatives, reading lists of names and praying for them. My impression is that the field of Thanatos, like other fields, can be experienced as either negative and chaotic (which I was feeling in my un-mourned state), and positive, when a supportive, communitarian atmosphere (a periodic attractor) is present.

I stayed on at the housing project for an additional year after its sale and then for two years in Chicago as a member of a formation team, prior of the community and a part-time instructor at Depaul Univ. and an instructor in church history and Psychology & Religion for a diaconate formation program. I have come to realize that it has taken at least these three years and maybe more for me to get over the trauma of the sale of the housing project and all that went along with that, including a very hate-filled atmosphere or field at the project due to groups vying for influence and power and in the process defaming those they perceived as enemies.

One of the basic archetypes of the personal unconscious is "persona." I haven't gone into this much in this work, but I'm sure that's an archetype we all have in common and one that is problematic for many. If "persona" is a word (mask) being used to connote a person's public face, the kind of image they would like to project to others, then that's something we all have to deal with. And like other psychic entities, persona too can possess people. I find myself, especially when around strangers, being rather intent on creating the "right" impression. Sometimes I even kind of freeze-up: an indication that the archetype is just not working correctly. It's certainly natural and important to want to give a good impression. But to be preoccupied inordinately with what others might be thinking about oneself, indicates a kind of possession by the archetype

My own experience of "persona" is mixed in at times with people-pleasing behavior. And that's often connected with a desire to avoid conflict. I guess the secret to breaking this kind of a pattern lies in consciously catching myself as this is going on, and deliberately taking some time out. I know that I at times study others to try getting a sense of their reactions to my "performance." I also know that when I am not doing this that I feel much freer and can express myself much more openly and honestly. Sometimes my inner conversation is very critical of others and engages in making irrational judgments and comparisons. Of course, that's not only *persona* stuff, but it can lead in that direction by making me want to look better than others at something. Heightened consciousness (not always easy to maintain), can help a person avoid showing off and it can help with humility as well. That's a word I like a lot because it reminds me to seek closeness to the earth (humus) and not get into a self-importance kind of field. And humility was just about the principal virtue Augustine always stressed.

I want to return to the subject of "synchronicity" again. A couple of nights ago I had a dream in which I was driving very fast on a freeway and I ran into another car from behind, sending it spinning up off the road and then crashing down on its top. I stopped and ran over to the crushed auto, and then awoke. Since I had the dream, I imagine there's information therein for me. However, the next day after the dream, a good friend left me a phone message to the effect that he was driving very fast on a freeway and as he was exiting that he had to break quickly in order to avoid hitting some cars that had stopped. I thought to myself: "Now this might also be a dream for my friend." So I called him and related the dream to him, suggesting he be more careful in his driving. He was aware that he needed to work on leaving earlier for his appointments and, in general, that his driving was at times reckless. This dream presents both me and my friend with a kind of synchronicity.

A phrase that is presently getting my attention is "soul-making." And I think it's getting my attention because being in touch with synchronicities helps bring about the experience of soul-making. By that term, I mean feeling alive, being interested in things, enjoying relating, seeing value in one's work, and, in general, experiencing something of the interconnectedness of all things and of one's own integrity. It has to do with feeling comfortable in one's own skin and believing that one's present path and trajectory are "what is wanted." So it has to do with destiny, with vocation, with individuation and with authentic belonging. And as I write this section, that's what I'm feeling: soul-making in all the senses I've just described. It's rather pleasant having this experience of the Muse or the Transcendent Function or Synchronicity at play here.

I am reminded of the Hebrews who, having escaped from captivity in Egypt, longed to return there because they couldn't stand the uncertainty of the desert. Or Jesus' disciples Peter, James and John, who were so taken with a Theophanous event on Mt. Tabor where Moses and Elias appeared with Jesus, that they wanted to stay up there and settle down. I am viewing those events as metaphors for the frequent experience people have of grasping onto some idea, or place, or person, or movement, as though it were the final and definitive answer to everything. I am admitting that tendency in myself. Like, here's some convergence indicated by way of synchronicity, and my mind immediately wants to cling to this as the final word. What I am realizing is the process and quantum ephemeral nature of synchronicity: you think you have a handle on it, and suddenly it's off and running like a wave, rather than a particle that will hold still. This is the pilgrim life, a kind of not-knowing definitively yet open to the wind of the Spirit. Ego keeps trying to jump in there to take control but something or someone is already and sufficiently in control.

I went back and reviewed a two-page handout I wrote up as a guide to presenting this study. It does give a kind of bird's-eye view of the whole paper, but I think for a group discussion we're planning that I will simply hand it out (the guide), and then allude to it, and whoever is interested can read it at their leisure, and then go right into this chapter wherein I get into more personal and feeling-toned material which has had an impact on me. I have noticed in giving talks, whether as part of church services or otherwise, that if I lead in with only abstract material, I loose the participants. On the other hand, if I lead with a personal story or more concrete visually stimulating anecdotes, that people are with me, and then, eventually, I can get more abstract if that's necessary.

Also, it seems to me that the "incarnation" within a presenter of concepts like synchronicity, have much more real teaching value and are far more impacting, than abstractions. And as a presenter, I must admit that I feel much more energized dealing with the visual and the personal even if my ultimate goal is the transmission of some kind of message of a more abstract nature.

I was reading somewhere about "lucid dreaming," which means that the dreamer is conscious enough to direct the dream figures to do his or her bidding. I imagine a person can seek to manipulate synchronicities that way too, by consciously and in an ego-centered kind of way, interfering during these experiences by claiming personal responsibility for them. This sort of stance would say that the synchronicity experience did not come as grace from the transcendent but rather was an invention of one's ego. I don't think lucid dreaming is a good idea, nor, of course, is claiming to be the source of synchronicities. In both cases one is interfering with an attempt on the part of Self (the divine), to grace someone. Now it may well happen that the deeper currents of one's unconscious feel very much attuned to the hints and movements of synchronicity. That would certainly be a blessing and is not the same as ego interference.

I am herein thinking aloud, or at least in writing. This evening I am going to speak with some teenagers on the developmental archetypes (see Pearson and Pearson & Marr). I had them do the PMAI instrument, so now we'll try to do some understanding and interpreting of the results. All the kids I'll be with are equally comfortable in English and Spanish, but since the instrument is in English, I plan on mostly staying in that language system. What do I want to accomplish with the teenagers? I'd hope that they will be able to describe in their own words each archetype, have some grasp of what archetypes are, and be able to articulate patterns they see each in his or her own case, from doing the instrument. That's a tall order, so I may have to meet with them more then once. These kids are Juniors and Seniors in high school and they would all be culturally in a kind of in-between place: not completely culturally Mexican like their parents and grandparents, and certainly not mainstream Mexican Americans, and not Chicanos either, which is more of a descriptive term for more activist and militant Mexican Americans who feel disaffected from both cultures. So these teenagers are a unique bunch, whether they know it or not, and I suspect they don't. They tend to party on the other side of the border, and the boys have more freedom of movement in that regard than the girls. They tend not to hang out with non-Latino kids, and, although they understand my Spanish, I struggle to understand their dialect, which is a kind of border patois or "jerga." Of course, it's not unusual for teenagers to develop a self-specific language, but this one is at times incomprehensible to me and probably pretty difficult for their parents too.

I've made use of the developmental archetypes as a way to understand the several populations of any group or institution. Recall that these archetypes can be divided and re-combined in several ways, and the principal way is by using the metaphor of the Hero's Journey and seeing the archetypes as three groups of four: preparation for the journey, the journey and return. In conjunction with Quantum theory, I, as the author/organizer of this material, would want to ask myself, "What is my interest in this about?"

The last time (during Sept., 2007) I did the instrument to determine personal developmental archetypes, I noticed that I was fairly high in most categories, but very low comparatively in the archetype of Orphan. The first archetype is this schema is that of Innocent, and that of course is related to the Orphan. The Innocent has to do with developing a sense that basically life is trustworthy and the world a safe place; then one gets disillusioned with too rosy a picture, difficult and disillusioning things happen, and a sense of life not being so trustworthy and the world not so safe, begin to move into one's psyche. If a person can successfully navigate through this and then come to the conclusion and realization that both things are true: sometimes the world is safe and life is supportive, and sometimes not; and then begin to adopt the conviction: "whatever the case, how I do and how I survive is largely up to me, so I'd best get to it because nobody's going to do it for me."

I can visually remember when this latter aspect described above of the Orphan archetype first hit me. I was sitting at the dining room table doing homework. It was for a history class, and the teacher's name was John Sullivan (an excellent teacher). I was in third year high school. I recall that while details were important for this teacher, dates, names, etc., that mostly he stressed patterns and movements. Anyway, I suddenly realized that I liked the class and the subject and that I wanted to do well in it, and then I just concluded that if I were going to do well in school and get into whatever that thing was called "college," that I'd better study and study hard, and that it really was up to me. I was very ambitious money-wise at that time, and always had several little jobs going on so I could have some income. And now (really it felt like a quantum leap), I was getting serious about studies. It was shortly after this that I also started thinking seriously about the college seminary and seeking to join the religious order known as the Augustinians.

My ponderings about myself and the Orphan archetype lead me to believe that my low score has to do with that part of the archetype which gets a person not to be too optimistic about things, that there are bad people out there, and that sometimes others may cause you harm or at least wish you harm. Anyway, that's just a little self-analysis in trying to understand why my score for this archetype deviated so much from the rest of the scores. And I do think I have had, for good and for ill, a bit of a naive and overly optimistic view of human nature and of individual people. So that all gives me some food for thought and I'll see how I do with the Orphan the next time I take the instrument.

It would be interesting to have the focusing ability to self-analyze on the basis of each of the twelve developmental archetypes. Probably that's easier in a group setting so one doesn't have to be the designated "client" all the time. I hope I can help get the kids in the youth group here at least curious about figuring out why they scored whatever they did in some of the categories.

F. David Peat writes as follows in Synchronicity,

"...Jung believed it is only within the objective layers of the mind, deep below the level of personal repressions, that the energies and patterns of synchronicity are to be found. Indeed, the deeper we dig into the mind the more we discover that the distinction between mind and matter is dissolved and the operation of the objective intelligence begins to manifest its power." (p. 99)

That again points to the fact that true synchronicity does not have its source in the ego, but, rather, in the non-ego, the Self, the organizing principle of the individual and of everything else as well. If one were pretty sure that the Self is arranging things along certain lines, then it would be very foolish to go against that movement. It is from the Self and when one lives in creative dialogical relationship with Self, that one experiences meaning in life. To not live in relation to the Self is to invite alienation and chaos.

Recently I had a dream in which I was getting ready to preside at Mass with a group. We were near the ocean, and just as we were getting organized for the service, I noticed that from way out at sea there was a huge wave coming. I had time to warn everybody and we all headed for higher ground and so escaped the wave's destructive power. I can recall a few other times when I've had tidal wave dreams. I don't recall in the former dreams that there were other people involved, and I think they occurred during times of great stress and when feeling personally overwhelmed. I'm not feeling that way right now, so I wonder about the dream: am I overwhelmed but just not in touch with the feelings? Or is perhaps the dream meant for some other person or group and I am merely the conduit? I know that the group assisting at Mass has been going through some difficulties lately. Another possibility is that I am picking up on some members of the group who are feeling overwhelmed by events impacting them, even if as a whole they are not experiencing any great catastrophe. I did decide to call one of the group's leaders due to the dream.

I organized a day of reflection around this writing for the first Saturday of Jan., 2008, in L.A., at one of a dream group member's home. Looks like the by-invitation group will number about 12. I plan on reproducing for the event just this chapter of the study and stressing the idea that it can be very energizing getting in touch with the unconscious, and that two related ways for doing that are dreams and synchronicity. And, hopefully, the people participating in the session will be able and willing to share some of their experiences along these lines.

Even as I was writing the above paragraph, the idea struck me that the group membership tends to gravitate more to the rational (thinking/sensation) side of things, and that among many members there is a tendency toward scientific exactness and precision (the NT personality type), and that the more feeling-oriented and NF (Meaning Seekers) are somewhat in the descendent. Is that what the dream is about: that a portion of them (or maybe mostly myself), is feeling marginated and overwhelmed due to the predominance and outspokenness of the more directive leadership-oriented thinking types? In any grouping or organization, the ideal is to have a balance of all the psychological types and developmental archetypes. None is better than another but when things get too far out of proportion, there could be trouble. Perhaps there's some need also right now in the community for more Jester energy to help keep the group from taking itself too seriously.

I am coming to the view that this section of my paper is, for me, the most life-giving and interesting as well. I don't know for sure why it took me so long to arrive at this point of actually applying Quantum theory to myself. It might well be similar to the fact that Augustine's Confessions have always been the most appealing and popular of his works, because people can identify with his experiences and so learn from them. Maybe I simply had to spend a lot of time with the theory first, and stay safely objective and uninvolved. And maybe there was a significant amount of fear in all this, in admitting that the primary application is to myself, even when I imagine myself being a kind of distant, objective observer. And, of course, in the Quantum world, there is no such thing as the objective observer; we are, all of us, always participants.

I want to mention that one of the most important things I've been learning over the years, and even more graphically in recent months, is that often one's body is wiser than one's mind. Put another way, I find I can get kind of mesmerized into thinking that all is well but when my body starts getting my attention through various ailments and pains, then I know something is not right. Recently I have had lots of foot and leg pain and difficulty walking. I went to a specialist (a podiatrist) and she eventually was able to create some inserts for my shoes that have completely eliminated the foot pain I'd been having. But now, with a bit of retrospect, I can see that my feet were telling me that it was time to move on; or, more accurately, my body was saying that something is not quite right. Eventually, "with a little help from my friends," I came to see that my living and working arrangements were not corresponding well to my system.

I think finding one's own "niche" is really important. And the body is a good reader of that. Paying attention to one's organism and responding to its comfort or ailments is a very basic way of showing respect to the anima/animus archetype. And, of course, all the archetypes have one foot in the body and one in the soul, so neither body nor soul can be left out or ignored, except at one's peril. I'd like to be more conscious of this. I'm also aware of missing two very important and, for me, interconnected experiences: interactive, dialogical learning in a community setting and experiences of the divine through prayer and worship with that community, with which I hope to reconnect.

On a more positive note, in pondering how I would like to spend my remaining years in work and ministry, I've come to the conclusion that what I most enjoy and appreciate is educating formation personnel involved in ministry training and education and, other ministry groups, such as in diaconate formation programs, in the psycho/social realities described in this paper. The intention of the participants would be mostly just the love of learning and the experience of community. I think that briefly sums up my bliss.

During the writing of this paper I feel I've been dancing around a content and method useful for a kind of holistic spiritual and psychological growth. I want to sum that up here as a way to end this chapter. This is simplistic, but I like to think that we people consist of enfleshed spirit. Looked at from one perspective, this spirit is psyche; looked at from another perspective, it is soul. In doing inner work with psyche, one is enhancing soul, and in paying attention to soul, as through prayer and sacraments and work for justice, one is also enhancing psyche. Clearly, a deep, intentional, prayerful and playful sacramental life lived in accord with one's religious tradition is one's response to the invitation by the divine to a life of gracedness.

On the psyche side, where we ourselves can take the initiative, we can, if we are able and if we so desire, pay close attention to our complexes, to our fantasies and dreams and to the archetypal fields which seem to both pass through us and at times hold us tightly in their clutches, both for good and for ill. And we can learn to pay attention to our compulsions because they can teach us about our ways of escaping whatever it is we are refusing to look at, acknowledge and deal with.

In all the above ways of "inner work" (see Johnson, 1986) I think dreams are really the key element. They are the voice of the unconscious. It is their images and archetypal powers we seek to run from by our complexes and compulsions and by the intricate weavings of our projections and introjections. As one looks at and seeks to have some communication with dream images, and tries to translate their strange symbolic language of images into a modern language, one is in effect communicating with the unconscious. And even if one gets the translation wrong at times, the mere act of showing a willingness to so communicate, to speak and to respond and to seek understanding, is enough to lay the groundwork for that healing that psychology calls the Transcendent Function and that religion calls the Holy Spirit. Dreams are like sub-atomic elements (part too of the Quantum Paradigm), because they won't hold still either and they lead the dreamer all over the place leaving traces also, like bosons and fermions, but now of psychological rather than physical fields.

Many organizations go through periodic reviews and self-studies that usually lead to some sort of certification. These evaluative studies are for the most part Newtonian and quantitative and stress measurable objectives. I don't know if any of the participants of these studies enjoy them, maybe some, but I suspect that most of the people involved in them see them as a necessary evil. What is not so common, in fact, hardly existing at all, is a qualitative study out of the Quantum side of things. I organized such a study of a housing project and found that the process and results were much more to my liking than the measurable kind. I suppose that's due in great part to the fact that I am more of a Quantum kind of a person than a Newtonian, although theoretically I can see the benefits of both approaches.

Corlett and Pearson in their book Mapping the Organizational Psyche, provide a clear method for doing a depth, qualitative analysis of an organization. In effect they ask the reader to consider an organization as a person, and suggest that one use the same categories one would use in doing a personal depth analysis. That means establishing who in the organization are the "ego," and then having this ego determine the psychological typology of the organization, describe its persona, determine what its four faces look like together with a distribution of the developmental archetypes, investigate the organization's complexes, and all with a view to determining how good a fit there is between the organizational ego and the organizational Self. So from the outset the organizational ego will have to determine what its Self is like.

This kind of a study will not yield measurable objectives, and so will probably not appeal much to the more Newtonian-oriented members of the organization studied. But it will yield a picture and reveal patterns and fields and it will surface sufficient data so as to make clear how large a gap there might be between what the Self of the organization is after, and what the ego of the organization has been about, and what it now needs to do to bridge that gap. The organizational ego will also need to check out their organization from the perspective of masculine/feminine energy, looking to see how much of a balance exists in the organization between these energies, and look for ways to move the organization toward a better balance if that is needed. Another central concern is finding out the quality of communication in the organization, both internal and with constituents.

I would like sometime to see this methodology applied to a parish. Like other organizations, parishes are often examined to check out such measurables as their financial status, participation by different ethnic groups, its gender and age make-up, numbers of baptisms, marriages and other sacraments, etc. These evaluations yield valuable information. But it's rare for a parish, or any organization, to undergo a depth, qualitative evaluation such as the one briefly described above. I think the reason for that is the prevailing prejudice that if you can't measure something, there's no sense dealing with it. I hope this study helps dissipate that prejudice. I would be of the opinion that a Quantum analysis is just as valuable as a quantitative, measurable one. Each approach simply looks at an organization from a different perspective. I think a parish that would engage in a Quantum analysis would stir up a lot of interest in its parishioners and to the extent that there is broad participation in the study, that morale and a sense of ownership would increase among both staff and parishioners.

On a trip to Egypt to visit a friend in Cairo and get some sense of Egyptian monasticism and history, my friend took me to several monasteries, most of them quite ancient even at least one having roots going back to St. Antony the Hermit. We also went to visit and spend some time at a relatively new monastic site about half way on the main road from Cairo to Alexandria. This foundation is called "Sepphoris." It comprises several acres of land and many monastic buildings. There is a convent of nuns there and one Coptic monk who is also a priest. A Coptic bishop oversees the foundation, but being a bishop of a distant diocese as well, he's not often on site and the resident priest is responsible for practical management. I was impressed with the place because they are philosophically very ecumenical and open to admitting for shorter or longer time periods as the case may be, people of all or no faiths. When we visited, there was a group of

Swedish Lutherans there for an extended stay, some Copts, some Catholics and some Muslims. This is remarkable because the Coptic Church in general has not been particularly ecumenical even with Catholic Coptic Christians.

Anyway, my main point here in this writing is to see a similarity between what they are doing now at Sepphoris and what the early 13th century Augustinian movement did. The Augustinians didn't have large plots of land and so take people in to live a hermetical or monastic life with them. But they did form lay groups called Third Orders to live an Augustinian life in the towns and cities of Europe. They didn't share the same monastic space with nuns (as certain Benedictine men did in some foundations in medieval Europe and as Irish monasticism did) but they did help establish convents of Augustinian nuns. And one can also see today some of the Coptic Sepphoris ecumenical spirit in Augustinian foundations such as San Gimigano which is located in Tuscany near Florence, in their efforts to accommodate pilgrims and incorporate them to some extent into their common life.

Going to spend time at a monastic retreat center like Sepphoris or even looking to join a religious order like the Augustinians, people know that they are going into the unknown in many respects. At the same time I think it's true to assume that most people are looking for companions along the way with whom they can feel comfortable. What follows here from Penney Peirce is a good insight on this:

"The more you honor people as souls, the more you'll be able to hold differences as interesting and valuable. You'll feel connected to people you never thought you'd like. As you find similarities to more people, you'll understand the deeply cooperative nature of souls working together in both visible and invisible groups. We all belong to a group of souls who are parallel to us in development—a soul group—, which in physics' terms is really a resonant field of awareness based on a particular energy frequency. A soul group, then, is a cluster of beings that have evolved to a common frequency, which means they often have matching philosophies, knowledge levels, and motivation. These like-minded people may look like siblings or have similar upbringings, interests, life transitions, goals, or even names. They may be friends, family, colleagues, or nonphysical beings in higher dimensions. When you meet them you feel profound relief or excitement; you feel that you already know them and naturally want to like them no matter what." Peirce, Penney (2009-01-25). Frequency (pp. 248-249). Simon & Schuster, Inc.. Kindle Edition.

Studying Augustinian history and spirituality at the Augustinian Spirituality Institute gave me a new appreciation of the missionary efforts many provinces of the Order have engaged in, in particular the Spanish Province of the Philippines, the Irish Province, the Provinces of Italy and of Malta and more recently the Australian Province. Missionary efforts ultimately have the effect of also blessing the sending provinces generally and the missionaries individually. In fact, I think most returning missionaries would testify that they have received more than they have given.

The Future of the Order

Re. the thrust of the Order into the future: based on present numbers of students at the several levels of study and preparation, it would appear that Africa, the Philippines, and Latin America show the most promise in terms of numbers.

Greater communication among the provinces and other circumscriptions of the Order is necessary for the equitable sharing of resources.

The Augustinian Volunteer program of the Villanova province is proving to be a good way to keep the Augustinian spirit going among young people. The same can be said of the holding of Augustinian youth encounters.

I think the methodology of seeking vocations being employed by the Augustinians of the California Province holds much promise. And it does so because in conformity with the psychology of the place. What people are looking for (at least in California, Oregon and Washington state), as they look into the possibility of a vocation, is a place to call home. They might like the idea of religious garb and a stylized and formal prayer life, but that is not the same thing as wanting great formality or institutionalization. The craving is, rather, it seems to me, for the personal within the continuity of a tradition. So the personal touch of phone calls, invitations to dinner, to participation, in some form, of a religious community life at the formation house on Cole Street or some other local community, is really appreciated.

Gaudium et Spes of Vatican II emphasized the idea that religious congregations need to up-date themselves and join modernity. More recently people joining religious orders want to restore the symbols many had left behind. One can best see this in the "movements." In a way this trend defies liberal/conservative categories. One manifestation of this is a desire to bring back the Latin Liturgy. Yet the same person who wants to wear a habit might or might not be traditional in his or her theology. Maybe too a younger generation is looking for ways to be distinguished from middle class values. It is true that religious today in more affluent countries live a middle class or even upper class lifestyle. In Africa the preoccupation of the people is rather how available are the priests to us? Are they being of service to us? Expectations differ from culture to culture and even place-to-place. Like human beings, religious orders also have a life cycle. It has foundation, expansion and stabilization; then in a critical period extinction, minimal survival and revitalization. Originally, Mendicancy was the dominant of religious orders including the Augustinians; then there was expansion all over Europe; by the 16th century, breakdown. And this pattern has repeated itself several times. The Order may well still be in crisis, but it seems it is seeing a new dominant image for our times. For example, in 2010, there were 2, 610 solemnly professed Augustinians; at the same time, slightly less than 100 novices. Is there a present dominant image for religious life? Yes: fraternal, conventual, and contemplative. Add to these certain more traditional hopes about the group one want to join, all of which is connected to a desire for home and family life. They generally want to find love and a sense of fraternity. This brings up the question: can one live alone and still be a member in good standing in the community? That's of course not the ideal but sometimes circumstances and needs of various kinds make that an option.

What makes an impression on people, however, both on those in a community setting, and those who observe them, is the living together "seeking one heart and one mind intent upon God," after the example set in the Acts of the Apostles. This is really powerful witness and it is seen and experienced within an operative and vibrant paradigm of grace. Recall that my thesis in this paper is that living this way and consciously being aware of the many archetypal forces in interaction in the community is the way the old patriarchal paradigm will be eventually nudged aside. Attempts to attack the paradigm directly simply give it more power.

So religious are looking today for a balance between conventual life and apostolate. This mixed ideal is profoundly Augustinian, and from Augustine himself. He even insisted that his own diocesan clergy be single and live in community. Augustinian foundations out of an Irish heritage tend to put the emphasis on apostolate. The continental European model is tending more toward the conventual side. Perhaps the present crisis in vocations to religious life and priesthood has something to do with this. I mean that some people would be turned off because they don't perceive much of a dynamic prayer and contemplative life in our communities, and some others because they don't perceive in us much of a commitment to the most poor and alienated. A Quantum paradigm would unrelentingly insist on both.

In the early missions of the Augustinians there's no evidence that they thought of the natives as any less than fully human. Some members of other orders did have this concept. They did think they had a calling to civilize them, esp. those of the lowest classes. So they sought to civilize esp. those who lived outside the cities. Now to "civilize" meant propagating a Spanish way of life. The Augustinians went to the mountains, the jungles, etc., with the intent to Christianize. The Augustinians first mastered the many languages of their area. In1534 (they arrived in 1533) they had a chapter. Each friar had to choose one cultural group to work with. They also trained catechists, a role not existing in Europe. They promoted devotions esp. to Mary, the Eucharist and processions. They also tried to introduce the natives to contemplative life.

and became involved in social assistance. They were entrusted with large encomiendas, and on this basis the friars could take care of the basic needs of the local population. I recall visiting Acolman Augustinian monastery near Mexico City some forty years ago. I hear it's been restored since, but then I could see it also served as a fortress in which the local people could seek refuge when attacked by hostile tribes.

Another characteristic of Augustinian spirituality is a willingness to share one's life with people of many different cultures and languages. Right now I'm in Rome at St. Monica's College and I hear conversations in French, Italian, Swahili, Spanish, Maltese, Tagalog, English, and many other languages. I think this points to another characteristic of Augustinian spirituality: the universal call to brotherhood/sisterhood. The reason I mention this (aside from my fascination with languages) is to point out the great need we all have in our world that people of different cultures, languages, customs, etc., might live together in peace, and that they not just tolerate each other, but celebrate their diversity while seeking to act together in unity for a better world. So in that sense this piece of Augustinian spirituality is something many people can be encouraged to emulate.

For a spirituality to qualify as Quantum it would have to be taking as many things into account as it possibly can: prayer together, focus on both interiority and mission for justice, embracing of cultural differences, a willingness to assist one another in the quest for wholeness and holiness, a dedication to continuing education, delight in each other's company, and, perhaps, making use of a method such as outlined in this paper as Jung's map of the soul/psyche such that the archetypes and their interactions within each person and between the members of the community are looked at with an eye toward spotting growth or decline. So archetypal movements can be used practically to give a community some indication of individual and group health. And all this with a firm conviction that grace is always operative and that when faced with insurmountable difficulties the members of the community can admit their individual and collective powerlessness.

I want to return for a moment to something I was commenting on in the chapter on Education and that is a kind of confession that I have a history of great difficulty attending classes. I do much better experientially when I am in the role of teacher. I recall even back in college (some 50+ years ago) going into a kind of stupor during class sessions, even when I was interested in the subject. Once for a few weeks I brought vials of smelling salts, ammonia based I think, and I would occasionally whiff them to keep myself alert. I became quite ill for a while from that practice and stopped. But here I am, with several academic degrees and lots of interest in many topics, and I am confessing that attending formal classes has been for me a monumental penance. I must be taking that into account when I teach because I use a lot of visuals and try to introduce variety into a class session. I go more into the theories of education I like and try to adhere to in the Education chapter of this paper. This also makes me wonder if I perhaps have some kind of learning disorder.

I found it a great shock when I had a diagnosis of leukemia in 1990. But I seem to no longer have it to any great degree. I suppose it was mainly the word itself I found scary. Then in the summer of 2011, I found out I had diabetes; again something of a shock, but it is s quite controllable with diet and medication. And I'm doing fairly well based on the self-testing I do. Sometimes I can't help but wonder if it is one of these ailments that causes me to have intermittent insomnia. But then on reflection this has been for me a perennial problem for as long as I can remember. I have concluded that this is just one of those things I can't handle alone, so I confess a powerlessness over it and just commend myself to the Lord in this respect. I decided to stop imbibing alcoholic drinks in about 1992, and began an internship at a treatment center for religious men and clergy. So I learned some things about AA, among them this notion of powerlessness. I think Jung came up with the notion and suggested it to the founders of AA as one of the 12 steps because he was influenced by Augustine's doctrine of grace. At least that's a suspicion I have. Whether it was or not, I think it's a concept that very much matches the way things really are: that we humans are not as self-sufficient as we'd like to think we are, and that our emotional, psychological and spiritual survival depend on our recognition of that, and of our need to admit powerlessness over many aspects of our lives, not just with respect to our addictions. Aside from this being part of my personal reflections, I am going into this again here out of a conviction that any Quantum paradigm has to include the notion of powerlessness and of the reality of grace, that that's just the way reality works.

Time for another confession: my weakest psychological function is sensation. The class we had at the spirituality course in Rome on iconography I found quite challenging. Yet I really enjoyed it and found I got pleasantly lost while doing slow and detailed work (inferior function) on the icon. It was as though I was accessing lots of stored up energy. I consider that for me that's "opus contra naturam" which can be both challenging and rewarding at the same time.

I want my reflections to include the observation that both St. Paul and St. Augustine (especially based on what I just wrote about powerlessness and relying on grace) were both predecessors of modern depth psychology.

15
CONCLUSION

Underlying all reality is interaction/relationship and the interplay of sub-atomic particles, and archetypes and their fields. The experiencing of archetypes gives life flavor as does prayer and contemplation and the experience of God's indwelling presence (which, by the way, also stirs up and constellates archetypal forces). Consciousness of archetypal constellations in one's life and the ability to name and work with them and understand their meaning, brings a zest to life and work, to spirituality, ministry in general and spiritual and pastoral counseling. One can sort out the working and effects of grace ontologically from the interactions of archetypes, but experientially they are all mixed up, as if God had become human and were flavoring the archetypal. Which is now the nature of things; God is not to be equated with Self but Self is experienced *as if* God.

It is possible, and desirable, to get in the habit of regularly looking within to see what archetypes are at work and what they might want, and to feel their presence physically also. To avoid looking at them or to not want to relate to them or include them within one's interactional field, will inevitably bring staleness and boredom and maybe even illness. While God's grace is not archetypal since it does not have its source in the creation, one can *experience* it as archetypal through the experience of the Self. And this experience of grace is salvific.

That God's grace and the experience of the divine are experientially inseparable from the archetypal ought not surprise the Christian since, according to the doctrine of the Incarnation, God in Christ got all mixed up in the human condition and according to the doctrine of the Ascension will always remain so. So archetypes, among other things, also mediate the divine to us. They are not divine but they are experienced *as if* they were.

If one hopes to see the patriarchal paradigm diminish and a new one emerge, I think it's clear from this paper that one would live as completely as possible in and out of an Augustinian spirituality or something very much like it, and that one would encourage others to do likewise. There are many Augustinian Secular groups and other affiliates and Augustinian-sponsored groups and movements that we can also encourage to adopt this spirituality if they haven't already done so, and maybe even the conscious use of archetypes as well as a kind of specific method in spirituality. There's probably nothing better one can do than this as a way to participate in the birthing of a more holistic and life-centered paradigm for our time. And since the core of this spirituality is "community," one would want to offer some concrete suggestions about how to live community in the context of one's real life.

For Augustinians the community is a place of learning. This "learning" is more learning for life than specific content. Communities don't just naturally happen, they are produced by intentionality. The central concept is that community members become committed to each other and to their communal and personal growth. Augustine imagined community as a place of cohesive and collaborative learning. There are also the "least" in a community context. Living like this one learns humility. So one gets in touch with both an outer and an inner Teacher. One discovers in ways that enable one to keep on searching (De Trinitate 9:1). This learning is a restless journey. The best way to do this searching is through dialectic and conversation.

Summary

I've aimed at presenting some details of a new sort of paradigm or world-view, which might provide a common ground for people of all spiritualities. I've shown how the activity of people interacting with each other, with themselves and with other aspects of creation is a reflection of the great loving source of all life we call God. I have suggested that the Strange Attractor at work seeking a new order out of chaos is "community," a variant of which is a desire for participation in general in something larger than oneself. I think the reader will appreciate that with "community" as the strange attractor, Augustinian spirituality is, in effect, counter-cultural on many levels, including with regard to the paradigm of patriarchy.

I have suggested some phenomena of which to be wary and others to deliberately seek as one consciously endeavors to collaborate in the on-going process of creation, in particular that of admitting powerlessness and so living in Christ. I have wanted to give a religious twist to my ponderings, especially by concentrating on the Augustinian notion of God's ever-present grace. This study is basically out of the field of Social Psychology and Archetypal Pattern Analysis as well as out of Augustinian Studies and Spirituality.

On p. 20 of Quantum Theology O'Murchu writes: "We'll get to the future in each other's arms -- across all the divides of race, creed, and culture -- or otherwise we may not get there at all." And that's what paper is, ultimately, all about.

"The new sciences could be effective sources of wisdom in modern society. They could inspire greater solidarity in the human world, and greater concern with and care for the natural environment. They confirm that our fleeting impressions and intuitions of oneness are not figments of the imagination but have roots in the reality of the cosmos. We are indeed one with each other, with the living world, and with the universe at large, for we are subtly but effectively connected. Our individual actions, and even our thoughts and intentions, affect other people around us, and are affected in turn by other people. This makes us part of a network of connection and wholeness. With this realization we could become part of the solution rather than remaining part of the problem. We could become moral agents seeking wholeness in

as well as around us; conscious architects of a sustainable planetary civilization."
(P.15, Lazlo, 2006, *Kosmos*).

Definition of the Holon

The "Holon" is the central metaphor in the New Paradigm (Quantum Theology). Considering every aspect of creation: the material, the psychological, the social and the organizational, everything is tied together as one great vibrating web. The Holon is specified everywhere in the web through interaction/relationship; through chaos and re-organization; through darkness (shadow) and light; and through archetypes and their fields. And holding it all together is the interaction/relationship of cosmic love that is the divine.

We share the same beautiful yet challenging world and our future depends, in no small part, on our getting on well together and recognizing that there's more that unites than that separates us. May we all be united in as many ways as possible, especially in relationships of friendship in community.

A Dream

A second large church is being built next to and connected with the old one. The interior is roughly finished and has the look of a huge cave. A group of women are preparing a kind of symposium at the church. The general subject is "women in the early church" and the "place of women in Christian Gnostic communities." I want to participate. I notice Fr. X is there in the audience with his religious garb on. I wonder if he will have something to say. I get in line to offer my thoughts. The man ahead of me seems to not take the proceedings very seriously and is just quoting authors without saying how they are relevant to the subject.

Among other things, I think this is a "wish" dream. While I don't see any psychology taking the place of religious systems, I do believe that psychology (and a Quantum Psychology in particular), can leaven the churches into being more faithful to their foundational and seminal values as well as helping them up-date their approaches. From Jesus' teachings, one of the seminal and foundational values of the Christian movement was great regard and respect for women. The paleo-Christians were forgetting this or repressing it in order to conform to the Empire values of patriarchy in order to be accepted. The dream also hints at the importance of speaking one's own truth rather than just quoting others. Maybe this dream will have some meaning for you too. Maybe it's one of those "big dreams." Those are dreams that come to people, not just for their sake, but also for a larger culture of which they are a part.

At the beginning of this paper I offered the following as the Dominant of the study: *summaries of theories of the social, psychological, theological and quantum sciences, especially concentrating on archetypal field theory and Augustinian spirituality and their connection with Quantum thought, are presented, with a view toward articulating a holistic view of reality and the pressing need to move toward more collaborative ways of being.*

To expand somewhat on that statement, what I've wanted to do is show how interaction, and particularly interaction involving archetypes on the human level, has to do with the most fundamental of personal and social realities; and that as a consequence of that fact, that we really need to pay close attention to the activity of archetypes. We have looked at the archetypes and their fields from many perspectives: education, psychology, communication, religion and theology, the new sciences and planning, to name a few.

I am convinced that the most basic source of conflict among people stems from whether a person is fundamentally Quantum or Newtonian. What I mean is that some people who are strongly living out of the Yang energy (Newtonian) side of things are at times deeply disturbed by people who are living out of Yin (Quantum) energy. Each feels threatened by the other and sometimes each will jump to the conclusion that the other is fundamentally flawed, acting in bad faith, or otherwise and somehow a threat to good order. From the Yang point of view, the Other is too soft and understanding and inclusive; from the Yin point of view, the Other is too hard, despotic, closed-minded and intolerant. Politically this comes out frequently in populations moving either toward fascism or toward a sort of chaotic socialism. Eventually, though, even socialism becomes fascistic if it gets too intolerant.

But more personalistically, when anyone is too embedded in one extreme or the other, the opposite is experienced as the "enemy." *They are corrupt and corrupters, crazy, to be eliminated at all costs.* A tragic example of this was the Spanish civil war (1936-1939) and its aftermath. The country was for a long time so polarized that one was considered either a nationalist or a subversive. And this is still being played out in many of our daily lives. I would suggest that if you have a very difficult time with someone and if the causes of this negative relationship don't seem to lie in differences of psychological temperament or personality, that you investigate the possibility that it stems from this more basic psychological field: that one person is Quantum and the other is Newtonian.

"I am circling around God, around the ancient tower, and I have been circling for a thousand years, and I still don't know if I am a falcon or a storm." Selected Poems of Rainer Maria Rilke (trans. by Robert Bly), San Francisco, Harper, 1981, 13.

I put this quote from Rilke on the front cover of this paper because it expresses something of my feelings in doing this writing. I've been engaged in this for about twenty years now. It hasn't been a linear or particularly logical an enterprise. Rather, I am swirling about, now adding in something here, and now something there and wondering if I am ever going to finish the project. At the same time, I've put together a series of power-point presentations as a way to put my thoughts together in an educational way and make the content of this paper more popularly palatable. My bliss, I must say, is more in that area than in the writing. And I love images more than abstractions and probably because images tend to awaken archetypes more vividly. By way of methodology, I think most learning in ministry preparation takes place during educational classroom sessions and "on the job." So I see this written text as more a reference or backup for that.

I want to end these reflections with one further contrast between the Newtonian and the Quantum universe. We are all always living in both worlds, but it is mostly the Quantum one which gives us the freedom to be creative and to deliberately have intentions about each other and our organizations. In other words, when in the world in a Quantum kind of way, we are shaping our futures for good or for ill. Quite a tremendous responsibility! Based on my dream above and seeing it as metaphorical, what are we going to do about Patriarchy, and our many secular and religious organizational severe Logos emphasis? Are we invested enough in our common future to consciously want a world and church more deeply imbued with Eros and Feeling? I believe it is possible through intentionality and specific actions to help bring that about.

I also believe that those who can move comfortably between the Newtonian and Quantum worlds will also be better able to navigate the sometimes turbulent waters between Donatus and Pelagius. One who gets stuck in Newton might well become too literalistic and activistic. One who gets stuck in Quantum might well become what euphemistically is called a "space cadet."

But ultimately, I think one must admit powerlessness in the face of such a daunting task. And this admission of powerlessness, Augustinian and Jungian as it is, means that such transformation is ultimately in God's hands, and will get worked out in God's time and through God's grace. The best one can do is await, become empowered through powerlessness, and prepare for the coming of the Reign of God by living the kind of life in community Jesus, the Acts of the Apostles, and later on Augustine, envisioned.

"Thou awakest us to delight in Thy praise; for Thou madest us for Thyself, and our heart is restless, until it repose in Thee." (The Confessions of Saint Augustine Kindle Edition, p. 1). More popularly: "You have made us for yourself O Lord, and our hearts are restless until they rest in you."

SOURCES AND SUGGESTED READINGS

*Indicates a more appropriate source for my course *Psicología evolutiva religiosa*.

*Adson, Patricia R., Ph.D., Depth Coaching, Gainesville, FL, CAPT, 2004.

Anonymous, Didache The Lord's Teaching Through the Twelve Apostles to the Nations, BooksAndSuch, Kindle Edition, Kindle Locations 3-4, 2009-12-16

Armstrong, Karen, The Bible, Atlantic Monthly Press, N.Y., 2007.

Armstrong, Thomas, Neurodiversity: Discovering the Extraordinary Gifts of Autism, ADHD, Dyslexia, and Other Brain Differences, Da Capo Press, Cambridge, MA, 2010.

Arnold, Patrick M., Wildmen, Warriors, and Kings (Masculine Spirituality and the Bible), Crossroad, N.Y., 1992.

*Augustine, St. Aurelius, Confessions, an electronic edition, text and commentary (c) 1992 by James J. O'Donnell.

Ibid. The Confessions of Saint Augustine, Kindle Edition

Ibid. Confessions, Second Edition, Translated by F. J. Sheed, Introduction by Peter Brown, Hackett Publishing. Kindle Edition. (2011-05-18).

Ibid., On Christian Doctrine (De Doctrina Christiana), Kindle Edition

Ibid., On Grace and Free Will, Kindle Edition

Ibid., The Trinity, introduction, translation and notes, Edmund Hill, O.P. editor John E. Rotelle, O.S.A.,New City Press. Kindle Edition, (2011-01-23).

Baggett, Jerome P., Sense of the Faithful (How American Catholics Live Their Faith), Oxford University Press, N.Y., 2009.

Barrow, John D., New Theories of Everything, Oxford Univ. Press, Oxford, 2007.

Barry, William A. & William J. Connolly, The Practice of Spiritual Direction (2nd edition), Harper One, N.Y., 2009.

Bateson, Gregory, Mind and Nature, Cresskill, N.J., Hampton Press, 2002.

Beck, Don Edward & Christopher C. Cowan, Spiral Dynamics, Malden, MA, Blackwell Publ., 1996.

Bell, James Stuart & Tracy Macon Sumner, Jesus, N.Y., Penguin, 2005.

Bible, Kindle Bible (KJV) (best navigation with Direct Verse Jump; paragraphed) [Kindle Edition]

Blumer, Herbert, Symbolic Interactionism; Perspective and Method, Englewood Cliffs, NJ, Prentice Hall, 1969.

Bly, Robert, Iron John, Addison-Wesley Publ. Co., Inc., N.Y., 1990.

Bohm, David, Quantum Physics: Bohmian Wave Mechanics / Wholeness and the Implicate Order (electronic articles), 2005.

Borg, Marcus, Jesus (Uncovering the Life, Teachings, and Relevance of a Religious Revolutionary), San Francisco, Harper, 2006.

Ibid., & John Dominick Crossan, The First Paul: Reclaiming the Radical Visionary Behind the Church's Conservative Icon, N.Y., Harper One, 2009.

Brent, Allen, A Political History of Early Christianity, Kindle Ed., 2009.

Breslin, Jimmy, The Church That Forgot Christ, N.Y., Free Press, 2004.

Briskin, Alan, The Stirring of Soul in the Workplace, San Francisco, CA, Berrett-Koehler Publ., Inc., 1998.

Cahalan, Kathleen A., Introducing the Practice of Ministry, Collegeville, Minnesota, The Liturgical Press, Kindle Edition, 2010-12-15.

Campbell, Joseph, Cfr. *Joseph Campbell Foundation*, an electronic website for articles and other publications and information.

Ibid., Pathways to Bliss, Novato, CA, New World Library, 2004.

Cannato, Judy, Radical Amazement (Contemplative Lessons From Black Holes, Supernovas, and Other Wonders of the Universe), Notre Dame, IN, Sorin Books, 2006.

Carroll, James, Constantine's Sword: The Church and the Jews, Boston, Houghton Mifflin, 2001.

Citro, Massimo, M.D., The Basic Code of the Universe (The Science of the Invisible in Physics, Medicine and Spirituality), Rochester VT, Park Street Press, 2011.

Collins, Dianne, Do You Quantum Think?, N.Y., Select Books, Inc., 2011.

*Conforti, Michael, Field, Form, and Fate: Patterns in Mind, Nature, and Psyche,

Woodstock, Conn., Spring Publications, 2003 (publ. in Italian as Il codice innato by Luciano Perez, Roma, Edizione Magi, 2005).

Ibid., Threshold Experiences, Brattleboro, VT, Assisi Institute Press, 2008.

*Corlett, John G. & Carol S. Pearson, Mapping the Organizational Psyche: A Jungian Theory of Organizational Dynamics and Change, Gainesville, FL, (CAPT: Center for Applications of Psychological Type), 2003.

Covey, Steven, The Seven Habits of Highly Effective People, N.Y., Fireside, 1989.

Crossan, John Dominick, God and Empire: Jesus Against Rome, Then and Now, N.Y., Harper One, 2007.

Dalai Lama & Victor Chan, The Wisdom of Forgiveness., N.Y., Riverhead Books, 2004.

Deutsch, David, The Fabric of Reality, N.Y., Penguin Books, 1997.

Dowd, Michael, Thank God for Evolution (How the Marriage of Science and Religion will Transform Your Life and Our World), Viking, N.Y., 2007.

Ehrman, Bart D., God's Problem, N.Y., Harper One, 2008.

Ibid., Jesus Interrupted: Revealing the Hidden Contradictions in the Bible (And Why We Don't Know About Them), N.Y., Harper One, 2009.

Epstein, Mark, M.D., Open to Desire, N.Y., Gotham Books, 2005.

Feiler, Bruce, Where God Was Born, N.Y., Harper Perennial, 2004.

Ferguson, Everett, Backgrounds of Early Christianity (3rd ed.), Grand Rapids, Michigan, William B. Eerdmans Publ. Co., 2003.

Feynman, Richard P., The Meaning of It All, Perseus Books, Reading Mass., 1998.

Ford, Kenneth W., The Quantum World (Quantum Physics for Everyone), Cambridge, Mass., Harvard Univ. Press, 2004.

Fox, Thomas C., Sexuality and Catholicism, N.Y., George Braziller, Inc., 1995.

*Frankl, Victor, Man's Search for Meaning, N.Y., Pocket Books, 1984.

*Freire, Paulo, Pedagogy of the Oppressed, N.Y., The Seabury Press, 2000.

Ibid., Pedagogy of Freedom, (trans. by Patrick Clarke), London, Bowman & Littlefield, 1998.

Funk, Robert Roy W. Hoover & the Jesus Seminar, The Five Gospels, N.Y., Polebridge Press (Scribner), 1993.

Giannini, John L., Compass of the Soul: Archetypal Guides to a Fuller Life, Gainesville, FL, CAPT, 2004.

Gonzalez, Justo L., The Story of Christianity (Vol. I, The Early Church to the Dawn of the Reformation), San Francisco, Harper Publ., 1984. (Also in Spanish)

Guy, Laurie, Introducing Early Christianity: a Topical Survey of its Life, Beliefs and Practices, Downers Grove, IL, InterVarsity Press, 2004.

Hawking, Stephen with Leonard Moldinow, A Briefer History of Time, N.Y., Bantam Books, 2005.

Hopcke, Robert H., Jung, Jungians & Homosexuality, Boston, Shambhala, 1991.

Holmes, Urban T. III, Spirituality for Ministry, Morehouse Publ., Harrisburg, PA, 1982.

Horsley, Richard A., Jesus and Empire: The Kingdom of God and the New World Disorder, Fortress Press, Minneapolis, 2003.

Hughes, Kevin L. Ph.D., Historia de la Iglesia, Loyola Press, Chicago, IL, 2005.

James, William, The Varieties of Religious Experience, Prometheus, 2002, N.Y. Originally published 1911).

Janz, Denis R. (General Editor), A People's History of Christianity, Fortress Press, Minneapolis, 2005-2009 (in seven volumes).

*Johnson, Robert, Inner Work: Using Dreams and Active Imagination for Personal Growth, Harper & Row, N.Y., 1986.

*Ibid., Harper Collins, Inc.. Kindle Edition.

Jung, Carl G., The Collected Works, (esp. *# XX, Psychological Types), Princeton, Princeton Univ. Press, 1990.

*Ibid., Memories, Dreams, Reflections, Vintage Books, N.Y., 1965.

Keen, Sam, Fire in the Belly, Bantam Books, N.Y., 1991.

*Keirsey, John & Marilyn Bates, Please Understand Me II, Prometheus Nemesis Book Co., Del Mar, CA., 1998.

Ibid., por favor, comprendeme, Tusquets editors, Mexico D.F., 2001.

Keller, M.A., *La vida religiosa en la experiencia y carisma de San Agustin*, en revista CONFER 97, (1986) 63-76.

Kelly, Dr. Robin, The Human Hologram: Living Your Life in Harmony with the Unified Field, Energy Psychology Press, Santa Rosa, CA, 2011.

*Kelsey, Morton, Dreams: The Dark Speech of the Spirit A Christian Interpretation), Doubleday & Co., N.Y., 1968.

*Ibid., The Other Side of Silence: A Guide to Christian Meditation, Paulist press, N.Y., 1976.

*Ibid., Prophetic Ministry, The Psychology and Spirituality of Pastoral Care, N.Y., Crossroad, 1982.

*Ibid., Reaching: The Journey to Fulfillment, San Francisco, Harper & Row, 1989.

*Ibid., Through Defeat to Victory (Stories and Meditations of Spiritual Rebirth), Element, Rockport, Mass., 1991.

*Ibid, Companions on the Inner Way, N.Y., Crossroads, 1995

*Kelsey, Morton T. & Barbara Kelsey, Sacrament of Sexuality, Amity House, Warwick, N.Y., 1986.

Kennedy, Kerry, Being Catholic Now, Crown Publ., N.Y., 2008.

Kipnis, Aaron R., Ph.D., Knights Without Armor, Jeremy P. Tarcher, Inc., L.A., CA, 1991.

Kirsch, Thomas, Virinia Beane Rutter & Thomas Singer (editors), Initiation: The Living Reality of an Archetype, N.Y., Routeledge, 2007.

Knox, Jean, Archetype, Attachment, Analysis (Jungian Psychology and the Emergent Mind, N.Y., Routeledge, 1993.

Laszlo, Ervin, Science and the Akashic Field (An Integral Theory of Everything), Rochester, VT, Inner Traditions, 2007.

Ibid., "Paths to Planetary Civilization," Kosmos, Vol.V, no.2, 2006, pp.12-15.

Ibid., The Chaos Point: The World at the Crossroads, Charlottsville, VA, Hampton Roads Publ. Co., 2006.

Ibid., Science and the Reenchantment of the Cosmos: The Rise of the Integral Vision of Reality, Inner Traditions, Bear & Company, Kindle Edition, Rochester, Vermont, 2009.

*Mark, Margaret & Carol S. Pearson, The Hero and the Outlaw, N.Y., McGraw-Hill, 2001.

Matkin, J. Michael, Early Christianity, N.Y., Penguin Group, 2008.

Maturana, Humberto R., & Francisco Varela, The Tree of Knowledge, Boston, Shambhala, 1998.

Mayer, Elizabeth Lloyd, Extraordinary Knowing: Science, Skepticism, and the Inexplicable Powers of the Human Mind, N.Y., Bantam Books, 2007.

*McBrien, Richard, The Church (The Evolution of Catholicism), Harper One, N.Y., 2008.

McTaggart, Lynne, The Bond: Connecting Through the Space Between Us, London, Hay House, 2011.

Miller, Arthur I., Jung, Pauli, and the Pursuit of a Scientific Obsession, N.Y., W.W. Norton & Co., 2009.

Moore, Thomas, The Soul of Sex, N.Y., Harper-Collins, 1998.

Ibid., Dark Nights of the Soul, N.Y., Gotham Books, 2004.

Moore, Robert & Douglas Gillette, The Lover Within, N.Y., William Morrow & Co., Inc., 1993.

Ibid., The King Within, William Morrow & Co., Inc., N.Y., 1992.

Nelson, James B., The Intimate Connection, Philadelphia, The Westminster Press, 19898.

Neumann, Erich, Depth Psychology and a New Ethic, Boston, Shambhala Publ. Co., 1990 (first English edition 1969).

Nouwen, Henri, with Michael J. Christensen and Rebecca J. Laird, Spiritual Formation (Following the Movements of the Spirit), N.Y., Harper One 2010.

O'Donnell, James J., Augustine, N.Y. Harper Collins, 2005.

Ibid., The Ruin of the Roman Empire, N.Y., Harper Collins, 2008,

*O'Murchu, Diarmuid, Quantum Theology, N.Y., Crossroad Classic, 1997.

Ibid., Ancestral Grace: Meeting God in Our Human Story, Maryknoll, N.Y., Orbis Books, 2008.

PAD, Summary of the Six Archetypes, Team Me, Kindle Location 4, Come Alive,

Kindle Edition.

Paloutzian, Raymond F., Invitation to the Psychology of Religion, Boston, Allyn & Bacon, 1996.

Ibid., Pathways of Chance, Pari, Italy, Pari Pub., 2007.

*Pearson, Carol, Awakening the Heroes Within, San Francisco, Harper, 1991.

*Pearson, Carol S. & Hugh K. Marr, Introduction to Archetypes, Gainesville, FL, CAPT, 2002.

Peat, F. David, Synchronicity, The Bridge Between Matter and Mind, New York, Bantam Books, 1987.

*Peirce, Penney, Frequency: the Power of Personal Vibration, Hillsboro, Oregon, Beyond Words, 2009.

Plato, The Republic, Translated by Benjamin Jowett, Public Domain Books, Kindle Edition, 2009-10-04.

Ibid., Timaeus, Charles River Editors, trans. by Jowett, Benjamin, Kindle, 2011-06-19.

Ibid. Plato, The Complete Works, trans by Benjamin Jowett, (2009-10-04).

Potter, Christopher, You Are Here: (A Portable History of the Universe), N.Y., Harper Perennial, 2009.

Powell, Diane Hennacy, The E S P Enigma: The Scientific Case for Psychic Phenomena, N.Y., Walker & Co., 2009.

Progoff, Ira, Jung, Synchronicity and Human Destiny, N.Y., Julian Press, 1973.

Prothero, Stephen, God is not One: The Eight Rival Religions That Run the World and Why Their Differences Matter, N.Y., Harper One, 2010.

Randall, Lisa, Warped Passages: Unraveling the Mysteries of the Universe's Hidden Dimensions, N.Y., Harper Perennial, 2005.

Richo, Unexpected Miracles (The Gift of Synchronicity and How to Open It), N.Y., Crossroad Publ. Co.,1998.

Roberts, Sam, Who We Are Now, N.Y., Henry Holt & Co., 2004.

*Robinson, John C., Death of a Hero, Birth of the Soul: Answering the Call of Midlife, Tulsa, Oklahoma, Council Oak Books,1997.

*Rogers, Carl R., A Way of Being, N.Y., Houghton Mifflin Co., 1980.

Rohr, Richard, Falling Upward: A Spirituality for the Twp Halves of Life, San Francisco, CA, Jossey-Bass, A Wiley Imprint (2011-04-01). Kindle Edition.

Rubin, Harriet, Dante In Love, N.Y., Simon & Schuster, 2004.

Sagan, Carl, The Demon-Haunted World, N.Y., Ballantine Books, 1996.

*Sanford, John, The Man Who Wrestled With God, N.Y., Paulist Press, 1970.

*Ibid., Invisible Partners, Mahwah, N.J., Paulist Press, 1980.

*Ibid., The Kingdom Within, N.Y., Harper Collins, 1987.

*Ibid., Mystical Christianity, A Psychological Commentary on the Gospel of John, N.Y., Crossroads, 1993.

Schwartz, Gary E. R., Linda G. S. Russek, The Living Energy Universe, Charlottesville, VA, Hampton Roads Publ. Co., 1999.

Schachter-Shalomi, Rabbi Zalman, Wrapped in Holy Flame: Teachings and Tales of the Hasidic Masters, San Francisco, CA, Jossey-Bass, 2003.

Segal, Robert A., Editor, The Blackwell Companion to the Study of Religion, Chichester, West Sussex, U.K., Wiley-Blackwell Publ., 2009

Segaller, Stephen & Merrill Berger, The Wisdom of the Dream, The World of C.G. Jung, Boston, Shambhala, 1990.

Sheldrake, Rupert, A New Science of Life: The Hypothesis of Morphic Resonance, Rochester, Vermont, Park Street Press, 1981.

Sheldrake, Rupert, Terence McKenna, & Ralph Abraham, Chaos, Creativity and Cosmic Consciousness, Rochester Vermont, Park Street Press, 1992.

Smith, Huston, The World Religions, San Francisco, Harper, 1958.

Smith, C. Michael, Jung and Shamanism in Dialogue: Retrieving the Soul/Retrieving the Sacred, N.Y., Paulist Press, 1997

Spoto, Angelo, Jung's Typology in Perspective, Boston, Sigo Press, 1989.

*Stein, Murray, Jung's Map of the Soul, Open Court, Chicago, IL, 2007.

Ibid., Kindle ed.

Stevens, Anthony, Archetypes, N.Y., Quill, 1983.

Ibid., Private Myths (dreams and dreaming), Cambridge, Mass., Harvard University Press, 1991.

Ibid., The Two Million-Year-Old Self, College Station, Texas A & M Univ. Press, 1993.

Ibid., Jung: A Very Short Introduction, N.Y., Oxford Univ. Press, 1994.

Ibid., Archetype Revisited (An Updated Natural History of the Self), Toronto, Inner City Books, 2003.

Talbot, Michael, The Holographic Universe, N.Y., Harper Perennial, 1991.

Tallman, Bruce, Archetypes for Spiritual Direction, N.Y., Paulist Press, 2005.

Tarnas, Richard, The Passion of the Western Mind: Understanding the Ideas That Have Shaped Our World View, N.Y., Ballantine Books, 1991.

Ibid., Cosmos and Psyche: Intimations of a new World View, N.Y., A Plume Book (Penguin), 2007.

Taylor, Charles, A Secular Age, Kindle Edition.

*Ulanov, Ann & Barry, Religion and the Unconscious, Philadelphia, The Westminster Press, 1975.

*Ibid., Primary Speech (A Psychology of Prayer), Atlanta, John Knox Press, 1982.

*Ibid., Transforming Sexuality (the Archetypal World of Anima and Animus), Boston, Shambhala Publications, 1994.

*Ulanov, Ann Belford, The Functioning Transcendent, Wilmette, IL, Chiron Publications, 1996.

*Ibid., &Alvin Dueck, The Living God and Our Living Psyche, Grand Rapids, Mich., William E. Eerdmans Publ. Co., 2008.

*Ibid., Finding Space (Winnicott, God, and Psychic Reality), Louisville, KY, Westminster John Knox Press, 2001

Ibid., Spiritual Aspects of Clinical Work, Einsiedeln, Daimon Verlag, 2004..

van der Post, Laurens, Jung and the Story of Our Time, N.Y., Vintage Press,1976.

Varela, Francisco J., Even Thompson & Eleanor Rosch, The Embodied Mind, Cambribge, Mass., MIT Press, 1993.

Vedral, Vlatko, <u>Decoding Reality: the universe as quantum information</u>, England, Oxford Univ. Press, 2010.

von Franz, Marie-Louise, <u>Alchemical Active Imagination</u>, Boston, Shambhala, 1997.

Ibid., <u>Archetypal Dimensions of the Psyche</u>, Boston, Shambhala, 1999.

Watzlawick, Paul, <u>The Language of Change</u>, N.Y., W.W. Norton & Co., 1978.

Wessels O.P., Cletus, <u>Jesus in the New Universe Story</u>, Orbis Books, Maryknoll, N.Y., 2006.

*Wheatley, Margaret, <u>Leadership and the New Science</u>, San Francisco, Berrett-Koehler, 1999.

Ibid., <u>Finding Our Way: Leadership For An Uncertain Future</u>, San Francisco, Barrett-Koehler, 2007.

*Whitmont, Edward C., <u>The Symbolic Quest</u>, Princeton, N.J., Princeton Univ. Press, 1979.

Williams, Rowan, <u>Writing in the Dust,</u>

Wiesel, Elie, <u>Sages and Dreamers</u>, N.Y., Simon and Schuster, 1991.

Wilber, Ken, <u>Integral Spirituality</u>, Boston, Integral Books, 2006

Wolf, Fred Alan, <u>The Dreaming Universe: A Mind-expanding Journey into the Realm Where Psyche and Physics Meet</u>, N.Y., Touchtone, 1994.

ABSTRACT

The Dominant of this study is: *summaries of theories of the social, psychological, theological and quantum sciences, especially concentrating on archetypal field theory and Augustinian spirituality and their connection with Quantum thought, are presented, with a view toward articulating a holistic view of reality and the pressing need to move toward more collaborative ways of being.*

Our world, its cultures, people and institutions are finding the patriarchal paradigm no longer adequate for our time. In fact, this paradigm is doing great damage to the planet and its people and their creations due to its ethos of domination and control. Gradually a new paradigm is coming to the fore, one that can be called "quantum" because it tries to take all reality into account, and because fundamental to this paradigm are archetypes, which by analogy behave similarly to sub-atomic entities. The contrast between and implications of two different mindsets, Newtonian and Quantum, are also central concerns of this paper.

The author has an interest throughout this study in investigating the unseen, the backstage aspects of the material and human drama, which can seem very chaotic. *Community* is seen as the "strange attractor" which we need to pay special attention to as we seek to do what we can to guide our world toward a more humane paradigm and in the hope that this new way of perceiving will nudge that of patriarchy out of the way.

I put forward Augustinian spirituality as the soul of a new paradigm, wherein there is prayer together, a desire to grow together fully as persons, with a willingness to help each other mutually in this task, and with a commitment to the poor and marginated. I am suggesting as fundamental to this paradigm that such a community get familiar with four different sets of archetypes: those of the human psyche (ego, persona, shadow, anima/animus, self), the psychological functions and attitudes (intuition, sensation, thinking, and feeling; introversion, extraversion, perception and judging); those more common archetypes (warrior, scholar, parent and child), and the developmental archetypes (innocent, orphan, warrior, caregiver, seeker, lover, destroyer, creator, ruler, magician, sage and jester). This can be a review of life, using these archetypes as ways to focus. In getting familiar with archetypes, one is deliberately and consciously relating with the unconscious and looking to develop, as far as possible, those archetypes not yet birthed to consciousness. Dreams and dream work are also central to this study.

Much of this paper has to do with the central importance of grace permeating the human condition and underlying the activity of archetypes, and the importance of admitting with some frequency one's own powerlessness when faced with addictions of various kinds and seemingly insurmountable problems and challenges, including the challenges involved in hoping for a new paradigm.

CPSIA information can be obtained
at www.ICGtesting.com
Printed in the USA
LVOW04s1123220816

501352LV00031B/634/P

9 781500 632649